THE
COMING BRIDE

by
David Jones

The Coming Bride

© Copyright 2014 David Jones

All scripture references are taken from the NIV version of the Bible,
unless otherwise noted.
Copyright © 1973,1978 International Bible society.
Published by Hodder & Stoughton.

ISBN 9 780995 738607

Published by Royston Bethel Community Church, Bride Ministries

Book design & formatted by Peanut Designs
www.pnutd.co.uk

Dedicated to

Carolyn, my perfect bride.

Foreword

Dave Jones is one of the best kept secrets in the body of Christ. Rarely have I met a man who has such a grip on a life changing truth. What God has taught him is released in this book. It should be required reading for every man and woman in the ministry today. Satan cannot have a bride so his attack is on Christ's bride. The Bible is a book about the bride. It starts with the story of the bride and ends with the grand crescendo of the marriage supper of the Lamb. The Spirit and the Bride say come. A minister who violates the Bride proves that they know nothing of the church, absolutely nothing. If Christ is your best friend and the church is His Bride, then you would never think of violating her. Pastor Dave's message is for the end time church. The Bride has made herself ready.

Dr. Cleddie Keith
Pastor of Pastors and a friend of the bridegroom.

The Coming Bride

'God made a woman...out of the man, and he brought her to the man.'
~ The Father

'A man will be united to his wife, and the two will become one flesh.'
~ Jesus

'The Spirit and the Bride say come.' **~ The Holy Spirit**

'This is now bone of my bones and flesh of my flesh; she shall be called woman.' **~ The Man**

'I am my beloveds and my beloved is mine.' **~ The Bride**

'I remember the devotion of your youth, how as a bride you loved me and followed me.' **~ Jeremiah**

'As a bridegroom rejoices over his bride, so your God will rejoice over you.' **~ Isaiah**

'The bride belongs to the bridegroom.' **~ John the Baptist**

'I promised you to one husband, to Christ, so that I might present you as a pure virgin to him.' **~ Paul**

Contents

Introduction

' "For this reason a man will leave his father and mother and be united to his wife, and the two will become one flesh." This is a profound mystery – but I am talking about Christ and the church.'

Eph. 5:31-32

*T*he Bible starts with a wedding and ends with a wedding. At the beginning of God's story is the Bride's creation and at the end of the book is her revelation and consummation. Between Genesis and Revelation the mystery of the Bride is unveiled. All the prophets understood the importance of the Bride. Perhaps the highest understanding given to the apostle Paul was the deep appreciation of the relationship between Christ and his church. In Ephesians, after giving much information regarding the nature and roles of husband and wife, he surprises his readers by stating that he is actually talking about Christ and his church. Whilst admitting that this is a profound mystery, he nevertheless equates the partnership between husband and wife as a direct 'type' and picture of the relationship between Christ and his church. The writer of Proverbs similarly confessed to the complex nature of this relationship stating that he could not fathom 'the way of a man with a maiden' because it was 'too amazing' for him to understand.[1] The story of the Bride is perhaps the greatest mystery in the Bible. It is God's great parable of the relationship between Jesus and his church.

As amazing as this mystery is, it is an undeniable and recurring theme in God's scriptures. The centrality and significance of the Bride can be seen to unfold throughout the Bible. She is pivotal to understanding the meaning of God's creation and is of primary importance for the completion and fulfilment of the divine purpose. The Bride is intimately involved in every aspect of God's plans and is portrayed as an essential pattern of something greater in his unfolding mission. The story of the woman is the hidden yet most desired entity in God's redemption strategy. Every age and dispensation emphasises this secret treasure closest to God's heart. Much has been written and preached concerning the men in the Bible, but the essential presence of the woman is often overlooked. Jesus, however, never overlooked any women in his creation, as he understood that they were a beautiful picture of the church: his coming Bride. These women represent the Bride that he came to save; the church that he loves and is coming back for.

From the foundational understanding that the woman is given as a metaphor for God's church, great revelation can be gleaned by examining the unique women throughout the Bible. The Scriptures portray the Bride's creation, deception, redemption, conflicts and fruitfulness. The women in God's word were loved by kings, revealed by prophets and

---

1   Prov. 30:18-19

needed by patriarchs. Each woman in God's great story reveals something unique concerning the nature of God's ultimate Bride, the church. Some of these women are good examples of the church and others are bad. There are far too many women in the Bible than can be looked at in this short book, but some of the most pertinent ones will be considered. By learning from these women of the past, believers of today can grasp their own value to God and develop a greater understanding of his divine purpose in obtaining a Bride for himself.

Much is written and taught concerning the many aspects of church life. How to build a church, grow a church and run a church are the main themes of most activity in the Christian world today. However, little is written concerning God's ultimate and most important purpose for his church. This purpose is revealed through understanding the mystery that is his Bride. She is not an organisation, institution, business, or corporation. She is his beloved spouse and must not to be handled and used by men as some kind of earthly commodity. The story of God's Bride is not a business strategy to be scrutinised, but a love song to be captivated by. A true husband does not marry his bride for her to be managed and controlled, but to be loved and cherished.[2] Every Pastor should treat the church in the same way that he would want another man to treat his wife. That is what Jesus expects. The story of these women in the Bible is the story of everyone who has heard the Bridegroom's voice and chosen to belong to Jesus Christ. This is the story of the Bride of Christ.

---

2   Eph. 5:25-33

1

The Bride is Created

'The LORD God said, "It is not good for the man to be alone. I will

make a helper suitable for him."'

Gen. 2:18

At the start of the Bible, in the book of Genesis, God presents prophetic patterns, which continue to be outworked through the rest of his scriptures. God begins by unveiling great mysteries, of which the greatest is the story of the Bridegroom and his Bride. Understanding the story of Adam and Eve is essential in beginning to grasp the deeper and more complex mystery of Christ and his church.

God begins the divine narrative by describing the unique creation of a bride for, 'Adam, the son of God.'[3] Just as, 'Adam...was a pattern of the one to come,'[4] so Eve is a pattern of the church that is to come. In the deep omniscient mind of the God, one of the greatest thoughts to ever occur was generated. He would make something so unique, so glorious and so beautiful that even the greatest beings in his creation would fail to fathom

---

3   Luke 3:38
4   Rom. 5:15

13

or grasp its complexities.[5] This creature would be something made in God's very image having a unique nature that would allow deity to dwell within it. God would create a Bride for his Son. From the creation of Adam's bride and throughout the unfolding history of their relationship, God sets forth a picture of the extraordinary blueprint for his creation. Father, Son and Holy Spirit will each play an equal and essential role in ensuring that this perfect Bride will be finished at the culmination of the age. This mysterious operation of the Trinity will reach its climax at the fulfilment of scripture when the full nature of his created Bride will be revealed.

God started his celestial endeavour by creating the first woman. She was the blue print and the prototype of the Bride who is to come. She will be the glorious wonder of his creation.

Adam's Sleep

Gen. 2:21 'So the LORD God caused the man to fall into a deep sleep.'
Before his bride could be created, Adam had to be put into a deep sleep. This was no mere natural sleep, but one that speaks of something more powerful. For Eve's life to be brought into being her future bridegroom was required to have his life suspended. Adam's life and activity would have to cease for a period of time in order for him obtain his greatest companion and helper. The image of the man being dead to the world around him, yet awakening to receive his bride is profound yet simple. It is a direct parallel of how Christ would obtain his church and shows the process of its creation.

---

5   1 Pet. 1:12

Jesus died to obtain his Bride. The church could not have been brought into existence in any other way. Without Christ's death there would be no Bride. The death of God's Son two thousand years ago on a wooden cross in Judea, is the most vital fact in human history. Without this sacrifice being made there was no possibility that anyone could ever belong to God. Jesus had to die in order for his Bride to live and he was willing to give up his life for her. There was no other way, as Jesus himself explained to his disciples, 'Did not the Christ have to suffer these things?'[6]

The first Adam's sleep for the creation of Eve was only a picture of the greater and unsurpassed sacrifice that 'the last Adam'[7] would make for his Bride. The mystery of the death of Christ has been

'Jesus had to die in order for his Bride to live.'

explored throughout the ages, but all eternity will not be long enough to search out its depths. Whilst dying on the cross Christ was thinking of his Bride. His final words, 'It is finished'[8] are recorded in the Greek language but Jesus spoke them in his native tongue of Aramaic. In Aramaic the word for finished is also the word for bride.[9] When Jesus declared that his work was completed he also proclaimed that he had finally purchased his Bride. His final breath revealed his heart's desire and the love of his life. Paul spoke for every living soul when he declared that through his death Jesus 'loved me and gave himself for me.'[10] A more recent recipient

---

6   Luke 24:26
7   1 Cor. 15:45
8.   John 19:30
9   The Aramiac word 'Kalah' means fulfilled, completed and finished, but can also be translated 'bride'
10   Gal. 2:20

of God's grace wrote 'Amazing love, how can it be, that thou my God should'st die for me?' Despite its great complexity, Jesus did indeed die for his Bride. His Bride knows this and celebrates it. And since Christ's sacrifice, every time his church meets she takes Holy Communion to recognise and proclaim this truth.[11]

Bride from His Open Side

Gen. 2:21 'while he was sleeping he took one of the man's ribs and closed up the place with flesh'

While Adam slept, Eve was created. And as Christ died, the church was brought into existence. The divine surgeon is very precise in describing the operation that was necessary to form the Bride. During Adam's sleep his side was opened up. Raw flesh, blood and water would have been visible and may have spilled onto the ground. The same action was perpetrated on the body of Jesus: as he hung on the cross, His side was opened up with a Roman spear thrust through the ribs of his corpse.[12] The body of the saviour was pierced and opened, just as the prophets had foretold.[13] In opening his flesh in this way, a sudden flow of blood and water spilled out. This clear and crimson stream 'flowed mingled down' from the side of Jesus, witnessed by all who stood at the cross. They saw a greater operation taking place than had occurred to Adam in the garden. Through the open side of Jesus his Bride was being created and the church was being born. In the same way that Jesus 'came by water

---

11   1 Cor. 11:26
12   John 19:34
13   Isaiah 53:5 & Zech. 12:10

and blood,' so his Bride would also be born of water and blood.[14]

Five hundred years before Christ's death Zechariah prophesied about it saying, 'on that day a fountain will be opened...to cleanse them from sin and impurity.'[15] For the church to exist she had to be born of both cleansing liquids that flowed from the open side of Jesus. The water, which symbolises baptism, cleanses the believer through repentance and, by faith, enables them to belong to God. The blood cleanses by atoning for their sin. The blood of Jesus was his very life; nothing is more precious to his Bride than this. Without the shedding of his blood the church would not have her sins removed and could never have become his Bride. Christ's blood was shed for his people and they can all now know they belong to him. All members of his church can declare that 'the blood of Jesus...purifies [them] from all sin.'[16]

Through the open side of Jesus the Bride was taken out. Her original existence began inside her bridegroom. God saw Eve even when she was still hidden and concealed in Adam. The Hebrew words for concealed and virgin are almost identical.[17] The phrase 'In Christ' is mentioned multiple times in the New Testament when referring to the foundational position of God's people. This is because, through God's wisdom, the Bride of Christ was 'in him before the creation of the world.'[18] It is the place of the Bride's authentic beginning and the source of her creation. No one can belong to God unless they first accept their position as being placed in him. His church was united with him at the time of his death in order

---

14   1 John 5:6
15   Zech. 13:1
16   1 John 1:7
17   In Hebrew the words are Alam and Almah
18   Eph. 1:4

to be completely united with him in his life.[19] Just as Eve originated from within Adam and was formed and moulded into his wife, so the church was created in Christ and is now being formed and shaped into his Bride.

Bride of His Bone

Gen. 2:22 'The Lord God made a woman from the rib he had taken out of the man.'

Adam was made through a combination of the dust of the earth and the breath of God, but when creating Eve God changed his method and adopted a totally unique procedure. Eve was not created by the same process of the previous creation, but from the bone of her bridegroom instead of dust. She was a special, new creation, fashioned from the already existing Adam and made in his image. Adam could literally state that Eve was 'bone of my bones and flesh of my flesh.'[20]

In the same way, the church was not born according to the old order of creation. Christ's Bride is not manufactured from the dust; she is created from the life of her Bridegroom. Believers in Christ are not born of natural descent but are supernaturally born of God.[21] They are born into God's kingdom from heaven by the Holy Spirit[22] and they now belong to a new creation.[23] They are part of Christ's body, share in his spiritual DNA and partake of his holy nature. Since her divine inception, the church is continually being moulded and transformed, from 'glory into glory,'

---

19   Rom. 6:5
20   Gen. 2:23
21   John 1:13
22   John 3:3
23   2 Cor. 5:17

to become the perfect Bride ready for Jesus.[24] This refining process is shaping and preparing her to be ready as God's Bride, perfectly adorned for her Bridegroom.

Bride brought to the Bridegroom

Gen. 2:22 'He brought her to the man.'

After Eve was created she was brought to Adam. She was not abandoned and left to fend for herself, wandering the earth having no idea of why she had been created. Adam was probably aware of what God was going to make for him, and undoubtedly co-operated in the process of Eve's creation. When Adam awoke from his sleep, he was waiting with eager anticipation for Eve to be brought to him. In the same way that Christ was resurrected and is awaiting his Bride to be taken to him. In contrast to Adam's awareness of the situation, Eve may have been confused about what was going on. Many in the church share a similar initial confusion when embarking upon their new life towards their Bridegroom.

During her first day in Eden Eve would have had many questions and would not have understood everything that was happening around her. Adam knew the names of all the animals, but Eve didn't even know the name of her bridegroom. So it is often true of all new believers in Christ, upon conversion they enter a new realm of life that can at first appear overwhelming and confusing. Their eyes have been opened to see different things, but require time to adjust to the new environment. Just like Eve, they need time to grasp the full implications and purpose of their newly acquired status. Whilst rejoicing in their new life, they

---

24   2 Cor. 3:18

may not grasp the essential purpose of why they have been brought into this new kingdom. Recognising that they now have a new life, they have to adjust their senses to the fact that they were not created to live an independent self-existence. They were created to belong to someone else and to be given to him as his Bride.

The good news for Eve was that God was alongside to take her to Adam. She did not have to worry about working everything out herself. The LORD was there to help, guide and introduce Eve to the bridegroom and to lead her into her destiny. She would soon discover that she had been created to share her husband's ruler-ship and dominion over all of God's creation.[25] This divinely orchestrated courtship would have been an exciting and romantic adventure for this couple. In a similar way the Holy Spirit is always present to bring the church to Jesus. He explains, guides, comforts, counsels and leads believers into a closer relationship with Jesus. The Holy Spirit lives within the church to make sure that she completes the process of transition from birth and creation, to betrothal and consummation. He helps her to understand the glorious inheritance that she now shares with God's Son. He will never leave her and will ensure that she inherits all the blessings of her Bridegroom just as Eve did with Adam.

---

[25]   Gen. 1:28

Leave to Cleave

Gen. 2:24 'For this reason a man will leave his father and mother and be united to his wife and they will become one flesh.'

Matt. 19:5-6 'the two will become one flesh. So they are no longer two but one.'

United with her husband at her creation, the Bride is to be reunited to him in an even greater and more profound way in the future. The destiny of the Bride is clearly stated at the beginning of her creation and confirmed and reinforced by the words of Jesus thousands of years later. Christ's Bride, the church, is also 'his body'[26] and she is to become one with her Bridegroom. This is not merely a parable but a profound spiritual reality and despite being mysterious, Christ is indeed 'one in body' with his Bride. They are not to be identified as separate but as united. Jesus was very clear about this emphasis. Man may often try to separate the two but God insists on consistently uniting Jesus with his Bride. Some attempt to establish theological differentiations between the Bride of Christ and the body of Christ, but God always aims for the two to become one. Jesus certainly saw his church as being one with him and his great prayer was that his Bride would be united with him.[27] Paul also makes it clear that Jesus loves his church as his Bride, and as his own body.[28] God is not pleased when people attempt to cut up, separate and dissect his Bride: he hates divorce.[29]

What is interesting about the original statement in Genesis to leave

---

26   Eph. 5:23
27   John 17:20-24
28   Eph. 5:28-32
29   Mal. 2:16

parents, is that Adam and Eve had none to leave. It must be seen that through this statement God was providing prophetic insight for the future understanding of the purpose of the Bride. She is called to leave everything of the old creation and be united to her Bridegroom in the new creation. The church is pictured as always being in the process of leaving to go and be with the Lord. She cannot hold back from this journey towards her Bridegroom, but must always move closer to him. Jesus reinforced this understanding when reminding his disciples, 'if anyone comes to me and does not hate his father and mother...he cannot be my disciple.'[30] Such a strong statement places great emphasis on the understanding that the Bride of Christ must be prepared to forsake anything that will hamper her from being united with Jesus.

From this beginning, as illustrated through the creation of Eve, the Bride is unveiled in pattern and purpose. Despite God's original creation being perfect, the deeper destiny of the Bride would become increasingly prophetic and enlightening throughout the unfolding scriptures. The rest of the Bible describes the growing mystery of the story of his Bride.

---

30   Luke 14:26

2

The Bride is Deceived

'God saw everything that he had made, and, behold, it was very good.'

Gen. 1:31

Eve's Perfection

*I*n forming Eve, God was revealing an essential principle concerning the ultimate purpose for his creation. He was pointing towards the destiny of the Bride. Although God created animals in pairs of male and female, initially Adam existed alone without a companion. Eve was not just another life form deposited into God's existing creation, but through her God was speaking of something unique and mysterious concerning the nature of mankind and its ultimate relationship to him. Through the picture of the woman, God is outworking the overall divine plan concerning the eternal destiny of his Bride. It is only at the grand finale of God's original creation that Eve makes her appearance and it could be assumed that the creation itself was merely a preparation and build up to her unveiling. In a parallel way this present age is also waiting in eager anticipation for

God's greatest creation, his church, to be revealed.[31] Eve finally arrived, and when she did, she was displayed as the perfect bride for the 'Son of God.'[32]

Just as Eve was called 'the mother of all the living,'[33] so all who receive new life now belong to God's church. Upon receiving her new life, Eve inherited everything that she could ever have wished for. She had the perfect husband in Adam, a man who had no bad habits or faults, as sin did not yet exist in their relationship. She had the perfect home living in Eden, a paradise where all her needs would be catered for. She also had the perfect future as God himself had spoken the promise of increase and fruitfulness over her life.[34] Despite all that she possessed, Eve was still deceived.

Many Christians must learn the lessons concerning Eve's situation or they will fall into similar temptations and sin. Belonging to Jesus Christ means they will ultimately obtain everything they could ever hope or dream. In Christ believers have the perfect Bridegroom, a sinless saviour in whom there is no fault. They have the perfect home in heaven and 'in Christ' as, by his Spirit, they dwell with him and he dwells with them.[35] The perfect future is also planned by their heavenly Father, in an eternal dwelling in Paradise as the Bride of Christ.

Nevertheless, many Christians still fall into deception just as Eve did. As a result, they can feel isolated from the close companionship of Christ and fail to appreciate the power and riches of the Kingdom of Heaven

---

31   Rom. 8:19
32   Luke 3:38
33   Gen. 3:20
34   Gen. 1:28-31
35   John 14:23

within them. Any 'fall' like Eve's can result in them losing their vision of Jesus, seeing instead only a future full of trouble and worries. Something has gone drastically wrong when this is the situation in the life of the church; she has been deceived.

The Coming Deception

1 Tim. 2:14 'Adam was not deceived; it was the woman who was deceived and became a sinner.'

2 Cor. 11:2 'I am jealous for you with a Godly jealousy. I promised you to one husband, to Christ, so that I might present you as a pure virgin to him. But I am afraid that just as Eve was deceived by the serpent's cunning, your minds may somehow be led astray from your sincere and pure devotion to Christ.'

Satan tells lies and he is very good at it. He succeeded in convincing Eve to believe she was missing out on something, even when she had all that she needed. He does the same to God's Bride today. He will blind the church to the wonderful nature of her relationship to Jesus in order to tempt her into acting according to carnal selfish desires. Unfortunately, Satan's lying tongue is never still. He has convinced many Christians and churches that they don't really have 'all things'[36] in Christ and that they need to look elsewhere for their satisfaction. It is a lie. Jesus is perfect and has everything the church needs. He has planned all things perfectly and the Bride's future with him is secure and certain. She will remain safe if she believes him and accepts she is his chosen Bride. Many people will slander and lie about Jesus and his motives towards his people, but those

---

36   Rom. 8:32

who truly know him trust his word and resist the deception of Satan.

Despite Christ's perfect love, some Christians can often lose their devotion to him. Having tasted the goodness of his love they can often desire something else in addition. There are always other trees available in the garden and their fruit can sometimes look very appealing. When people believe the lie that there is something more satisfying than Christ, they can lose their first love and fall into deception. The church needs to be aware of this and be able to identify the signs of such deception.

Stay Devoted

Acts 2:42 'They devoted themselves to the apostles teaching and to the fellowship, to the breaking of bread and to prayer.'

When the first church was passionately in love with her Bridegroom, they were devoted to him in very specific ways. Today, if the church's devotion to these same things has disappeared, she has already been deceived. A true believer loves hearing about Christ and loves his family. They enjoy talking to him in prayer and are thrilled to remember his love at the communion table. A devoted bride has no greater joy than to talk to, listen to, and spend time with her husband. If any of these things are diminishing in a church's life, it may already have fallen out of love with Christ and have become infatuated with other things. When this has occurred in a church it may indicate that 'their sensual desires [have] overcome their dedication to Christ...thus they bring judgement on themselves, because they have broken their first pledge.'[37] Their devotion will then often continue to diminish and they will look for another partner.

---

37   1 Tim. 5:11

Satan has deceived them into falling in love with something else. He hates devotion to Christ and schemes to use the Bride for himself.

Avoiding Deception

Matt. 24:4-5 'Jesus answered "watch out that no one deceives you. For many will come in my name, claiming 'I am the Christ,' and will deceive many."'

Perhaps the most important step in avoiding deception is recognising that it can come upon anyone in some measure. If it happened to the first bride, Eve, who did have perfection on earth, it will certainly present itself to today's church, which is surrounded by the sins of the world, the flesh and the devil. If Jesus had to warn his closest disciples to avoid deception, he certainly needs his church to be aware of it today.

'God gives many ministers to his church, but his Bride is never given to anyone except the Bridegroom.'

All must recognise that the Bridegroom instructed his Bride to watch and be aware. Many people will try to deceive her and there will be many false prophets around in the last days.[38] The Bride should always know the difference between a true minister and a false one. A true prophet is always a friend of the bridegroom[39] and they become smaller so that Jesus can grow larger. They point away from themselves towards the true lover of the church, Jesus. Counterfeit

---

38   Matt. 24:11
39   John 3:29

leaders, on the other hand, desire to use the church for themselves. They crave her love, devotion and attention because they want to take the Bride as their own possession. God gives many ministers to his church,[40] but his Bride is never given to anyone except the Bridegroom. She belongs only to Jesus. Genuine ministers understand this and warn his church very clearly that 'many deceivers have gone out into the world.'[41] Such deceivers are antichrists and should be easily identified by the true Bride. Jude informed the church that they wander around, feed only themselves and speak against authority.[42] Peter said that they will exploit people with fabricated stories, seduce the unstable and mouth empty boastful words that promise freedom but end in slavery.[43]

Today, such counterfeit ministers seduce the church and, unfortunately, many enjoy listening to their lies. The serpent still coils around the Bride and injects his venom today, just as he did in Eden. Jesus warned everyone about such activity, but he also sadly acknowledged that many would still be deceived. These deceived Christians are inflated with pride and crave celebrity style ministries. They are infatuated with charismatic personalities and addicted to their anointing rather than being devoted to the Anointed One.

Every church needs to watch and be careful in case it finds itself becoming obsessed with certain types of ministry and ministers. It must not seek and crave only the ministries that are spectacular – limited to signs and wonders – at the expense of more hidden sacrificial service that ushers

---

40   Eph. 4:11
41   2 John 1:7
42   Jude 8-13
43   2 Pet. 2:1-22

in the presence of the Lord. It is an unhealthy sign when people desire miracles rather than Jesus. The greatest 'anointed' minister around today is still only a friend of the Bridegroom and, if he is genuine, will always step away from centre stage so that Christ can take the Bride for himself. Only Christ can provide the full love that the church requires. The true Bride should not be seduced by the slick words, enchanting techniques or spectacular presentations of the platform performers of today. Her heart belongs to the Bridegroom and to him alone.

Recognise the Bridegroom's voice

Isaiah 53:9 'There was no deceit in his mouth'

Eve was deceived because she listened to the wrong voice. Much of what the serpent says today has elements of truth, but the Bride must listen to discern the tell-tale 'hiss' in his voice. The bridegroom's tongue knows no guile and only speaks truth with words full of grace. His sheep recognise their shepherd's call[44] as a faithful wife knows her husband's voice. A wife is aware of the things her beloved would say and she recognises words he wouldn't use. This is true of the Bride of Christ; she knows that her Lord does not promote himself by slandering others, as the serpent did in the garden. She immediately becomes suspicious when people twist God's word to suit themselves, as when Satan misquoted the Lord.[45] She tests every word to ensure its validity.

The faithful Church has learned to always check the source of any alleged word from God. The good Bride always consults her spouse. Today, sadly,

---

44   John 10:3,4
45   Gen. 3:1-5

many are too quick to believe any word that appeals to the lust of the flesh, the lust of the eyes, or the pride of life.[46] A wise person investigates the origin of every word and checks the author of every prophecy. Eve should have checked the validity of the Serpent's deceitful words before acting upon them, but the snake was such a persuasive speaker and he promised such good things that she was seduced, deceived, and gave birth to sin and death. Eve could have also checked with Adam to obtain another witness to the truth of the serpent's testimony, but she didn't, she wanted the fruit, so she took it.

Christians must ensure that any 'word from God' is in agreement with their Bridegroom's perfect will for them. He is the Bride's protector and he is the original and ultimate Word from the Father and he knows everything. Christ is the Truth and he always seeks to keep his loved ones from deception. Eve, however, didn't even ask Adam's opinion. Maybe she thought she already knew what he would say or perhaps she believed that her intellect was adequate so no second opinion was required. Maybe she reasoned that, because she understood the difference between right and wrong she did not require anyone to tell her what to do. Whatever she assumed, Eve was deceived. She did not test the word or the spirit behind it[47] and she was sold a lie that resulted in horrendous consequences for all humanity.

Eve should have waited instead of acting in haste. If Eve had patiently weighed the new information then she would have soon discovered its invalidity. The LORD himself would be walking through the garden in

---

46   1 John 2:16
47   1 John 4:1

32

the cool of that very day[48] and he could have answered her questions and revealed the deception. Waiting for the LORD to give confirmation to his word is a valuable procedure in keeping the church from deception. He always speaks to those who wait upon him and is willing to give greater clarity and revelation concerning genuine words from himself. He is in no hurry and so his Bride should not be either. God does not hassle or pressure his Bride to act independently, but gives her plenty of time to make important decisions. The wedding of the Lamb has been a long time in preparation, as he is fully aware that his Bride needs time to get ready. No one should give way to manipulative bullying or clever coercion, as this is not the way God works. If any voice is pressurising a believer to make impulsive decisions without allowing adequate time for prayer and consultation, it is unlikely to be the voice of God.

The Husband's Authority

Col. 3:19 'Husbands, love your wives and do not be harsh with them.

Why didn't Adam forbid his wife from talking to the serpent and why didn't he stop his wife from eating the fruit? Surely he was stronger than her and was he not the head of his house also? Instead, Adam appeared to do nothing. In observing aspects of their pre-curse relationship, a glimpse of a correct understanding of the use of authority within God's blueprint for marriage can be seen. In the beginning the marriage between Adam and Eve was uncorrupted by sin and their relationship enjoyed a simple purity unspoiled by any elements of control and manipulation. Adam and Eve cared for, helped and loved one another; the two had become

---

48   Gen. 3:8

one flesh. Adam was created before Eve and he did have knowledge that she was not aware of, but despite this his wife had total freedom within the relationship to think, choose and act independently. She was neither controlled nor manipulated by her husband. As a consequence of the fall, sin entered the relationship between man and wife creating disharmony and disunity. Conflict, contention and divorce were never included as part of God's original blueprint for marriage.[49] The legalistic concept of men ruling over and controlling women only appeared after deception within the first marriage occurred. It was a result of the curse of sin and was not present in the original marriage relationship.[50]

Unfortunately, because the deception of sin has now infected the world, many of God's children continue to have a false understanding of the appropriate use of authority within loving relationships. As a result, authority is regularly misused within the church. In God's original marriage, if Eve wanted Adam to use his authority, she was obliged to ask him to intervene. She did not expect him to force his opinion into every situation or overrule her freedom to choose. Adam only appeared to use his authority if his wife requested him to be involved. Concerning the forbidden fruit, she did not consult his authority on the issue and, consequently, he did not impose or enforce it. Many of God's people are likewise deceived today because they have accepted an unbiblical view of the correct use of authority. Some people make decisions wrongly assuming that their heavenly Bridegroom will jump in and overrule them if their decision is wrong. This is an immature understanding. Jesus loves

---

49   Matt. 19:8
50   Gen. 3:16

His Bride too much to forbid her the right to make her own choices. He will not force his opinion on His Bride; she must consult, choose and then ask for his will to be done.[51]

Jesus is the perfect husband: He does not wield his authority to control or manipulate his Bride. Christ waits to be asked into any relationship and even knocks at the door in order to be invited into his own church.[52] When the church neglects to seek and ask his opinion on issues, it opens itself up to the strong possibility of deception that may lead to improper action. This can lead to direct disobedience with the resulting failure being the church's responsibility. Just as Adam existed before Eve, Christ existed before his church. He is the beginning and end and knows everything. He will always allow his authority to be used correctly, but people must choose to submit to it and operate from within a loving relationship with him. Jesus seeks the consent of his people and his love for them will never be forced, even if they are his Bride. When it comes to working with his Bride, God's method is 'not by might, nor power, but by my Spirit says the Lord Almighty.'[53]

Today, many believers are deceived and eat the fruit of their own knowledge before ever allowing a higher authority to be invited into the situation. 'The spirit told me to do it' is often heard on the lips of God's people, which is sometimes a thin veneer for excusing their deceived carnal behaviour. Like Adam, many leaders often see God's people participating in activities that they know will cause harm, but understand and accept that their opinions and authority have not been called on. A

---

51   Matt. 6:9-10
52   Rev. 3:20
53   Zech.4:6

wise leader does not force their will over a believer's life. Unfortunately, as in the case of Adam and Eve, many leaders are only consulted after the fruit has already been eaten. At this point, the poison of the fruit has already started to take effect and their ability to help at this stage is limited. Fortunately, the true Bridegroom is not limited when it comes to dealing with the consequences of disobedience. Under the Old Testament law an unfaithful wife had to drink the consequences of her own sin and receive the curse in her own body.[54] Under the New Covenant Christ drank the cup of sin on behalf of his Bride and paid the penalty in his own body.[55] He dealt with sin once and for all and he tasted death for everyone. He died for his Bride, paying the ultimate price for the one he loved. His true Bride, knowing the love and sacrifice of her beloved, does not desire to taste that fruit again, she wisely allows his authority, opinion and will into all her decisions and asks for them daily.

Self-Deception

1 John 1:8-9. 'If we claim to be without sin, we deceive ourselves and the truth is not in us. If we confess our sins, he is faithful and just and will forgive us our sins and purify us from all unrighteousness.'

After Eve believed the lie of the serpent, she fell into another realm of deception: self-deception. Just like Eve, everyone's natural reaction to sin is to hide it. Eve's fear of being exposed was so horrendous to her that she embarked upon a system of hiding her problem. Firstly, she tried to cover it up by making garments of fig leaves. Secondly, she hid herself amongst

---

54   Numb. 5:11-31
55   Matt. 26:42

the trees and thirdly she blamed someone else for her predicament.[56]

Today the very same excuses for people's problems can be heard in the church. In the first instance many people just hope nobody knows about it. They sew their own fig leaves together and hope people don't examine their lives too closely. If people did investigate, they would see the nakedness between the cracks in the deceitful covering. When this approach doesn't work some people just run away and hide somewhere. They may move to another church or stay away from Christians altogether hoping that no one sees them or their sin. When this fails, as it inevitably does, they blame someone else for their problems. They often say that they refuse to come to church because it is full of hypocrites or they blame someone else for their behaviour. They may reason that if they hadn't been mistreated or overlooked, they wouldn't have reacted in the way that they did. They may believe that their Pastor did not care about them and did not give them enough help, so it's understandable that they are behaving in the way that they are. The excuses can become very elaborate, but the sin is still theirs. This cycle of excuses avoids the real issue and may continue in the lives of some believers for years. The Bride, when fallen from her relationship, has always used similar excuses, but it is self-deception. The longer someone stays in this deceived condition the less they become aware of the real truth that their hearts have become 'hardened by sin's deceitfulness.'[57] There is only one way for the cycle to be broken: the Bride must confess her sin, return to the Bridegroom and allow Jesus to sort it out.

---

56   Gen. 3:7-13
57   Heb. 3:13

Jesus will never robe His Bride in fig leaves. Despite the fact that some legalistic religions force a woman to be totally covered up, Christ's Church is never to be hidden away. She is the Glory of her husband and he wants to reveal her beauty to all creation.[58] The Bride never needs to resort to blaming people, as she knows her saviour took all the blame for her actions and has freed her from all sin. This is her confession. The true Bride is no longer self-deceived, but aware of her sin and confesses it freely, because she knows that the blood of her saviour has forgiven her and purified her from all unrighteousness.[59]

Deceit of this Life

Matt. 13:22 'The worries of this life and the deceitfulness of wealth choke it, making it unfruitful.'

Eve was called to be fruitful but her deception limited her fruitfulness. The church today often finds that her fruitfulness is greatly limited by believing the lies of this world. It is a sad truth that many people fail to be fruitful for Jesus simply because they have been deceived into seeking other things. What can be wrong with wealth? Nothing...and therein lies the deceit. Wealth is good, but good things are often deceiving. Today entire churches are running after good things instead of following their Saviour. Despite there being many good and handsome men in the world, a faithful bride's heart belongs only to her husband. Jesus has called us into relationship with him: to seek him,[60] to know him[61] and to love him.[62]

---

58   1 Cor. 11:7
59   1 John 1:9
60   Jer. 29:13
61   Phil. 3:10
62   Mark 12:30

Too many churches are acting like wives who are bored with their husband and they feel compelled to get involved with something more exciting. Some of these churches pile up activities and continual social events that do little to enhance the devotional life of Christians. They cram their lives with as many good things as possible because, apparently, Christ is not enough to satisfy their desires. Having committed their lives to Jesus they are now seeking satisfaction from countless other sources and denying the sufficiency of Christ's love. They have been deceived just like Eve. They have been robbed of a greater truth and may have believed the lie that godliness is a means to selfish satisfaction and financial gain.[63]

Christ is true wealth. Only in him can full satisfaction be found. When people say, 'but surely God wants me to be rich?' they ask a deceitful question, as it falsely assumes that the Bride doesn't already have eternal riches in Christ. Satan's great lie is in blinding a believer to the fact that they already have all things in Christ. Beware of seeking anything other than Christ and his kingdom.[64] Fame, success, and wealth, may just be counterfeits of the real and genuine riches that already exist in Christ. His Bride is not to store up riches on earth, but to acknowledge the true wealth in heaven. It is a sad irony that Eve already had what she was trying to obtain, but she was focusing on the wrong tree. She could have had the life Satan promised by going to the Tree of Life. This tree, which speaks of man's relationship to Christ, has all that the Bride needs. The deceit led to trouble and unfruitfulness. Deception always produces barrenness in the Bride, but as shall be seen in the life of Sarah, the Bride of Christ is destined to be fruitful.

---

63   1 Tim. 6:5
64   Matt. 6:33

3

The Fruitful Bride

'Look to Abraham your father, and to Sarah, who gave you birth.'
Isaiah 51:2

*M*illions of people of many different faiths revere Abraham, the man of faith. He is a highly significant figure in human history and a great father of faith. However, fewer people look to Sarah, his bride. This is interesting because Abraham had several children and through them birthed different nations,[65] but Sarah had only one child. It would be the child of his bride that would be the promised one and the blessed one, not the children of the other women. Abraham was the source of God's promised child but only if it came through his bride. If the bride was ignored then the future seed would not be born and the promise would fail. It could be said that God's promise was specifically connected to the seed of Sarah not merely the general children of Abraham.

Today we find many people focusing on Abraham, but ignoring his bride.

---

65   Gen. 16:4; 25:1-6

God did not do this. Some people desire great faith like Abraham, a great name like his, and want to be remembered for a tremendous legacy, just as he was. Others want their names recorded, their achievements recognised and their unique relationship with God acknowledged, but they are ignoring the most important aspect of their calling and ministry. The real issue of faith and ministry should be focused on whether the Bride is going to be fruitful. The question that needs to be continually asked is: what is a minister's responsibility to the Bride; what are they doing about fulfilling the promise for the church?

Abraham was not Barren

Romans 9:8-9 'It is not the natural children who are God's children, but it is the children of the promise who are regarded as Abraham's offspring. For this is how the promise was stated: "At the appointed time I will return, and Sarah will have a son."'

Abraham did not have difficulty in producing children; he was fertile and proved he could be fruitful. The problem was with his bride. It was the bride that was barren and it is the same today. The resurrection proved that the Bridegroom of the church is more than able to birth his new life. Jesus is alive and is 'bringing many sons and daughters to glory.'[66] The current issue of fruitfulness is specifically concerned with his Bride, the church. The question is not whether he can be fruitful, but whether his church is going to be fruitful? Are his people going to be fruitful for him or will they pass the responsibility onto someone else? God's life must come through his Bride. It is the church that must birth the life of Jesus,

---

66   Heb. 2:10

not some other organism.

Sarah's story is the story of the church. The same question of faith was presented to them both. It is not a question of whether the Bridegroom has life, but, rather, if believers will learn the lessons of Sarah and become the fruitful Bride he desires. Will the church believe, submit and obey as Sarah did? It is only by learning from her example of faith that believers can accomplish what she achieved, become fruitful and reproduce the life of God.

Life and blessing comes from the bridegroom

Gen 12:1-2 'The LORD had said to Abram..."I will make you into a great nation and I will bless you; I will make your name great and you will be a blessing.'"

God's original word of blessing and promise were given to Abram, (his former name), not Sarah. She may not even have been aware of the full implications of God's covenant to her husband at the beginning of her journey. It is a similar situation with many in the church. A believer's life begins with their Bridegroom: life is in Christ, not within themselves. Christ is their Word and their promise, he produces their life and only through their relationship to him will they inherit all things. Likewise, the Church inherits the blessings of God through her connection to Jesus. The nature of this relationship is parallel to that of Sarah and Abram. Sarah was Abram's wife and also his half-sister, and so it is with Jesus and his church. Christians belong to Christ through a binding betrothal covenant and they are also part of his family. They are 'bone of his bone and flesh of his flesh'[67] and they share his family DNA being 'born of God'.[68] Without this marriage and family relationship no one has any right to obtain life, inherit blessing or bear fruit for God.

The Bride's Journey

Gen. 12:5 'He took Sarai'

Sarai, (her former name), was being taken on a journey by her husband. She probably didn't know where she was going, but she still had to decide whether she would go. She had to leave her home and the familiar life she knew and follow her bridegroom to a place that God had promised. She undoubtedly had many concerns, questions, and fears. She may have been concerned that Abram had misheard God's voice or gone the wrong way. She may have questioned if it was worth the sacrifice and whether they really had to leave everything. But only faith in God

> *'Without serving the church, ministers have no real purpose, just as Abram had no future without Sarai.'*

and her bridegroom would answer her questions and calm her fears.

One thing Sarai knew was that she was being taken somewhere. This was not her plan or idea, but she was trusting in her husband to get her to the correct destination. The Bride of Christ must have the same attitude of faith today. Despite what some portray, believers do not know every detail about where, when or how they will obtain God's promises, but they can have faith in Jesus and trust him to do it. The church is going

---

67   Gen. 2:23
68   John 1:13

somewhere, it has been called forward, and it cannot stay where it is. Jesus has prepared the place for her and he is also the way to it. He is the gate, the way and the life. Every church must move forward to be where he is. Sarai would lose all her other family relationships during this journey, but she was the bride, Abram's most important possession and she would never be lost. Jesus will never lose his Church.

The Bride in the World

Gen.12:11-13 "I know what a beautiful woman you are. When the Egyptians see you, they will say, 'This is his wife.' Then they will kill me but will let you live. Say you are my sister, so that I will be treated well for your sake."

In scripture Egypt is always a representation of the world. Just as Egypt wanted to take Abram's bride for itself, so this world wants to use the church for its own benefit. Satan desires Christ's Bride to be placed in his harem and he demands that the church exists to please him and play its part in his society. Satan commands that the church must become part of his kingdom and establishment, just as Sarai should be placed in Pharaoh's Harem to be used by him for his own satisfaction. In this incident Sarai was placed in a position of grave danger and sadly many leaders fail, like Abraham, when they allow the church to be used by this world to satisfy the lusts of its king. The Bride is in danger when she is allowed to be open to the possibility of being impregnated by the seed of this world. Abram failed to acknowledge his true relationship to Sarai, just as many leaders fail to grasp their full responsibility to the church.

Without serving the church, ministers have no real purpose just as Abram had no future without Sarai. The Church is not merely the sibling and relative of Christ – it is much more than that – it is his beloved spouse. No man, including the king of Egypt, has permission to touch his Bride. She does not belong to this world and she is not here to satisfy its lusts. Just as Pharaoh was seriously punished for daring to touch Sarai, so shall any man incur God's wrath who dares to lay a finger on his Bride. 'Jealousy arouses a husbands fury, and he will show no mercy when he takes revenge.'[69]

This unfortunate course of events was not Sarai's fault. She was not suffering abuse from the world because she had misguidedly chosen to be too close to it. (Sarai's great granddaughter, Dinah,[70] would later make this mistake to her own great misfortune). Instead, Sarai was suffering due to the actions of other individuals who should have known better. Sadly, just as Sarai was misused, many in the church are let down by weak leadership. Believers should not take this too much to heart as everyone, at some stage in life, will be failed by someone they trust. Abram, great as he was, was only human. His chose to save his own skin at the expense of his wife's purity and today many servants of God choose to benefit themselves at the expense of God's church. Thankfully, the true Bridegroom never treats his Bride in such a way and he will never allow his beloved to be taken by the king of this world. Jesus did not seek to save his own skin, but allowed it to be scourged and beaten in order to protect his Bride. When the soldiers came for Jesus in the garden,

---

69   Prov. 6:34
70   Gen. 34:1-2

he protected his disciples and ordered that were not to be taken. He gave his own life in exchange for his Bride and paid the price for her in full. Pharaoh cannot have God's church as she is not of this world and belongs to heaven. The King of this world will not be allowed to impregnate the church with his seed; only Christ's life will be birthed through her.

Betrayed Again

Gen. 20:2 'He stayed in Gerar, and there Abraham said of his wife Sarah, "she is my sister." Then Abimelech king of Gerar sent for Sarah and took her.'

Despite all that Sarah had been through, another great test was still to come. Undoubtedly, she now felt more secure, as she lived in a safer place out of Egypt and in the land of promise. She had a new location, a new place of residence and a new lifestyle. She must have believed that Abraham had received true confirmation from God about the coming blessing. And surely the fullness of the promise was close at hand. She may have expected that everyone had now learned from the mistakes of the past and her future would be more settled and secure. It was at this point in her life that Sarah was betrayed again. This second act of betrayal must have been agonising and deeply hurtful.

Many people can overcome one betrayal, but this second abuse was far worse than the previous one in Egypt. This was not mistreatment in the world, but was abuse at Gerar, the Promised Land. Betrayal that occurs in a place of relative safety and security cuts very deeply. One of the most upsetting aspects in the life of many Christians is not that the world hurts them, but that some in the church have mistreated them. Again, Sarah was failed by someone who should have protected her, but those she trusted gave way to fear and allowed her to suffer in order protect themselves.

Anyone who experiences this kind of betrayal must look up, be strong and have faith in God. Despite being mistreated by the men in her life, there was someone else who was watching over Sarah: her heavenly Bridegroom. All believers can be assured that Christ is taking his Bride to himself and that no-one else is taking her for themselves. As shall be seen, no one touches the Bride of Christ and gets away with it.

Gen. 20:3 'But God came to Abimelech in a dream one night and said to him, "You are as good as dead because of the woman you have taken; she is a married woman."'

God always steps in when his beloved church is under threat. Earthly leaders may fail, but the heavenly Bridegroom will not. It is interesting to note, that in the dream God did not say to whom Sarah belonged, but merely that she was married. Perhaps he was hinting towards the fact that the Bride ultimately belongs to Christ and anyone who touches her will suffer his wrath. When Christ walked this earth he would never suffer a woman to be abused. Whether protecting a woman from being stoned to death,[71] or granting her freedom to minister, his command to everyone else was direct and clear, 'Leave her alone!'[72] In times when church leadership fails the children of God must always fix their gaze on the true lover of their souls, Jesus. He who watches over them will neither

---

71   John 8:10
72   John 12:7

slumber nor sleep.[73] The Bride will be protected and ultimately delivered.

The Bride is Free, not a Slave

Gal. 4:22. 'Abraham had two sons, one by the slave woman and the other
by the free woman'.

Sarah was a free woman and the Bride of Christ likewise enjoys such
real liberty.[74] Unfortunately, Sarah was also barren and had no children
and like many people of today she was prepared to jeopardise her future
freedom in order to obtain temporary satisfaction. She knew what God
had promised, but she desired quicker results. She wanted success at any
cost and was prepared to get it through illegitimate means. Sarah wanted
to achieve her objective more than she valued her own freedom and was
willing to allow Abraham to impregnate a slave woman, as long as she
could claim the credit. The bride was willing to give away her position of
freedom and allow slavery and bondage to take her place.

Gen. 16:2.'Sarai said to Abram "The LORD has kept me from having
children. Go, sleep with my maidservant; perhaps I can build a family
through her."'

Sarai's opinion, thinking and conclusion were all wrong. Everything she
said here was based on unbelief instead of faith and God has made it clear
that, 'anything that does not come from faith is sin.'[75] Like Job's bride,
people under pressure can make wrong confessions.[76] Unbelief always

---

73   Psalm 121:4
74   John 8:36
75   Rom. 14:23
76   Job 2:9

gives birth to sin. Sarai proceeded along a line of action that would produce pain and conflict for her and her family and, unfortunately, many follow her bad example.

Firstly, she reasoned that God did not want her to have children. This was not true, as God fully intended that Sarai would be fruitful. Christ has no greater desire than to see his Bride being fruitful. He will, however, take her through the test of faith before conception and birth. The test of barrenness will always come to God's Bride as Rebekah,[77] Rachael[78] and the Shunammite[79] would discover. Believers have to learn to trust God to produce his life through them. It cannot come through carnal understanding, nor does it come by human reasoning. Today, many members of the church follow the same erroneous reasoning of Sarai. 'God wants me to be sick' or 'God wants me to suffer,' are statements often heard from many people in his church. This is never God's desired end for his church. The heavenly Bridegroom always plans the best for his Bride.[80] He may take her through many trials in order to strengthen her faith, but his aim is always for her fruitfulness and perfection. The faithful church will ultimately overcome.[81]

Secondly, she decided on her own initiative what should be done. It is a very dangerous path when the church tells God what is to be done. Sarai hatched an idea, a plan, and a strategy to be fruitful, but it did not require any faith it just needed everyone to do what she suggested. Much activity in God's church follows this same disastrous methodology of

---

77   Gen. 25:21
78   Gen. 29:31
79   2 Kings 4:14
80   Jer. 29:11
81   Rev. 2:10-11

Sarai. It is sure sign of future trouble when a church stops waiting upon direction from God in favour of voicing its own ideas and planning its own projects. Faith in God cannot be circumvented and human logic is not faith. God does not ask for success at any price, but looks for the true ripening fruit of faith. Regrettably, Abram did what Sarai suggested and she got what she thought she wanted. The church must be very careful about what it demands; it may very well get it, even if it is the opposite of what God desired to give them. The desires of the human will can be very persistent and often prevail against weak leadership. A strong willed individual like Sarai will often get what she wants, but she may then live to regret it.

Thirdly, she falsely believed that any fruit was better than no fruit at all. The church today is full of this false humanistic logic. It throws itself into all kinds of projects and activities often using anybody to achieve anything. Sarai did not really care about Hagar; she just wanted to use her to fulfil her own ambition. In a similar way some churches treat people like slaves, as a means to an end, as though God was a taskmaster demanding results at any cost. Christ is not a slave owner; he is the Bridegroom of his church. He doesn't want to produce bondage by treating people like slaves. He desires a relationship with his people that births life and freedom through the Bride that he loves. The result of Sarai's actions would indeed birth results, but it would be the fruit of slavery, not freedom. Ishmael would be born as a result of this mentality. His people would not inherit the promise and they would be treated as enemies and outcasts of what God had originally planned for his people. Lastly, through this course of action, Sarai would be worse off than she was at the beginning. When the Bride uses carnal methods to achieve spiritual fruit the result is always a cycle of emptiness and bitterness. She finished off blaming Abraham for her own idea and for being despised by those she tried to help. She, in turn, would react in her frustration and bitterness by mistreating others[82]. Many today also blame other people for their lack of support when, in reality, they may be planning something that is not according to God's direction. Believers must learn these lessons from Sarai; otherwise they may make the same mistakes and produce similar fruit resulting in bitterness and mistreatment.

The Bride Renamed

Gen. 17:15-16. 'God also said to Abraham, "As for Sarai your wife, you are no longer to call her Sarai; her name will be Sarah. I will bless her and will surely give you a son by her. I will bless her so that she will be the mother of nations."'

*Abraham received the pro*mise again, but this time there was a radical new revelation contained within the blessing. God's promise must come through Sarai, his bride. Finally, after many long years of trying to work it out, Abraham understood that it is the Bride that is to birth the blessing, not him alone.

So many Christians, especially those in leadership, still need to learn this essential lesson. After receiving great promises from God they can waste many years trying to force the birth of their promise. They may quickly grasp that they have a calling, a gift and a ministry and so they try every possible way to ensure their gift bears fruit. They tell everyone about it,

---

82   Gen. 16:5-6

raise funds and promote their ministry wherever possible. Not feeling appreciated, they often move to another church where they will be more accepted. They try using Hagar because Sarah doesn't work. If no one gives them a platform, they will establish their own. They continue to publicise themselves and promote their own abilities until everyone is forced to accept that God has chosen them to be such a great blessing to everyone. When this doesn't work, they double their efforts and change their name so that their ministry looks even greater, sounds more fantastic and feels wonderful. After all, had not God himself called them to be a blessing?

The truth is that God had planned to bless them, but when someone embarks upon this course of action they have missed the point. It is the Bride who is to birth the blessing and never just an individual. It was not all about Abraham and any woman that he chose. Ministers of God are called to make the Bride fruitful, not themselves. Their greatest joy should be in the blessing that the church births, not in obtaining their own selfish ambition. God may eventually disown any ministry that is not focused on bringing blessing to and through the Bride. Christ died for his Bride in order for her to be fruitful, so that she would be the means of blessing to all nations. He breathed his Spirit into her and sent her into the world. You cannot bypass the Bride, God will not allow it and if anyone ignores his church, Jesus will ignore them.

After a hundred years, Abraham finally understood the importance of the Bride and that God's focus was on hi swife, not just on him. Sarai would be renamed Sarah. The breath of God, the 'H', would enter her and she would birth the blessing. Abraham would play his part in the conception, but the promised blessing and greatest joy would come through the Bride.

The Bride's Joy

Abraham Laughed.[83] *Sarah laughed.*[84] *Everyone laughed.*[85]

When told that his bride would be fruitful Abraham laughed. He could not believe it, as her womb had been dead for a long time. He acknowledged that God had spoken, but it was too incredible to grasp. God's purposes for his Bride are often too amazing to comprehend. Is it possible that a dead church could still be fruitful after so many years of decline, decay, conflict and internal problems? The answer to the problem is not located in the condition of the church, but more precisely in what the Lord has said and what his will is. Abraham may have wanted to keep the matter to himself due to thinking that his wife would never believe it. What he did, however, is arrange a meeting where God could speak to his wife in person. All good leaders follow his example and allow the church to hear God's voice for themselves.

When God turned up at Abraham's house in Genesis chapter eighteen, he spent time in communion with his friend, but the Lord had a more important assignment that day asking 'Where is the bride?' Jesus always wants direct communication with his church. At times, he speaks through his leaders and prophets, but his greatest desire is for direct communication with his Bride; and he wants her to hear his voice for herself. When he speaks the church often laughs, just like Sarah and tries to conceal her joy that God could be so good to her. She does not dare believe and hope

---

83   Gen. 17:17
84   Gen. 18:12
85   Gen. 21:6

for such wonderful blessing to come upon her, but it is true that the Bride will be fruitful. It could well be the case that she conceived on the very day that God's word was given to her, as at the same time the following year the child had arrived. Such is the goodness of God. His Bride will not be barren. The true church will bear fruit and fruit that will last and Jesus said that no one would take his joy from his Bride.[86]

When the bride became fruitful, everyone shared her joy. Abraham's entire household rejoiced. In the same way the servants in the Bridegroom's heavenly household rejoice when someone is born into the kingdom.[87] Through Sarah's womb would come some of the greatest people that have ever walked the earth. All nations have been blessed by her. Through this bride came Isaac the son of promise and through Isaac came the ultimate blessing that gave fullness of joy to the whole of mankind; Jesus Christ, the offspring of the woman.[88]

86   John 16:20-22
87   Luke 15:10
88   Gen. 3:15

4

The Quest for the Bride

'Go to my country, and my own relatives and get a wife for my son.'
Gen. 24:4

*C*hapter twenty-four of Genesis is the longest chapter in the book. It exclusively describes in great detail, God's preoccupation with ensuring the correct bride was obtained for the promised son. Abraham also had to get a bride for Isaac, his only son whom he loved.[89] His son had been born through the promise and provision of God, and the same son was taken to the top of mount Moriah to be sacrificed. After the heart wrenching drama on the mountain, the next stage in Isaac's life sees him receiving his bride.

Abraham's son is a direct foreshadowing of God's only begotten Son, Jesus Christ. As the son was a gift from God, so the Bride must also be from God. The son was with the father, but the bride was yet to come. Abraham would not rest until Isaac received his bride and God the Father

---

89   Gen. 22:2

will ensure that Jesus obtains his. His beloved son must have his beloved Bride. Abraham's desire was that Isaac would have the perfect partner to share in his blessing and the inheritance from God. He needed to send someone back to get the correct bride and bring her to the father's house, so that she could be given to the son. He had someone who could complete the task, the chief servant in his household, the unnamed messenger who he entrusted with all his wealth. This special person would embark upon the quest for the bride.

The Plan of the Trinity

Gen. 24: 2-4 'He said to the chief servant in his household, the one in charge of all that he had, "Put your hand under my thigh. I want you to swear by the LORD, the God of Heaven and the God of earth, that you will...get a wife for my son."'

Here is an illuminating scene: three separate but connected individuals, the father, son and unnamed messenger are seen embarking upon a unique expedition to obtain the perfect bride. It may sound an audacious plan with unrealistic expectations; however, it is a picture of the eternal plan of God. After Abraham had received his son back from the dead, he would now get a bride for him.[90] Jesus is also now back in the presence of his Father in heaven. He rose from the grave and is now heir of heaven and earth and all that belongs to the Father is his. He is victorious over all things, but his Father has planned for something even more astounding: He will ensure that he gets a Bride for him to share in his eternal glory. Like Abraham, the Father has despatched the trusted messenger to bring

---

90   Heb. 11:19

the Bride back to the Son. The messenger is the Holy Spirit and he will complete the task of bringing the Bride home because he never fails in his quest.

The Spirit has been sent

John 16:13-15 "When He, the Spirit of truth comes, he will guide you into all truth. He will not speak on His own; He will speak only what He hears, and He will tell you what is yet to come. He will bring glory to me by taking from what is mine and making it known to you. All that belongs to the Father is mine."

The Bride is not always aware of his presence, as he does not speak about himself. The Holy Spirit comes from the Father to bring glory back to the Son and the Son's glory is seen in his Bride.[91] He has come to tell the Bride about the Son and to counsel and persuade her to believe that the Father has chosen her and that the Son desires her. He is here to take her away to be with God and share the Son's life and inheritance. He has promised the Father that he will get a Bride for the Son and he will do it. He will succeed on his mission to bring the Bride just as Jesus succeeded on his mission to purchase her. The remaining mystery is who the Bride will be, what will she be like, how she will be recognised and, most important of all, whether she will come.

---

91   1 Cor. 11:7

The Bride will be related

Gen. 24:3-4 'you will not get a wife for my son from the daughters of the Canaanites, among whom I am living, but will go to my country, and my own relatives and get a wife for my son.'

Abraham's messenger knew what he was looking for: a bride that was different from the people of Canaan. The Bride of Christ will not be born of this world. She will be related to the Son and born of the Spirit[92] and born of God.[93] She will have his spiritual DNA and not the flesh of Canaan. The true Bride of Christ is not related to this earthly realm and does not love the things of the world. She should be easy to locate as her light should shine in the darkness. She will not be a worshipper of idols or addicted to the things of this life. She will be looking for something better and watching for the promise to be fulfilled that God gave to her ancestors. The Spirit of God is also still watching things and hovers above the earth, just as the dove from Noah's ark hovered above the waters of the flood. He will not rest on the corrupted things of this world, but he will approach and settle on the things that are holy and pure. He rested on Jesus at his baptism[94] and he came upon the church at hers.[95] He always rests on the true Bride, the pure Bride, the one cleansed from the things of this world. He sees the true inner life and condition of every heart. He always recognises those that belong to the family of God and he can clearly distinguish between them and the Canaanites.

---

92   John 3:8
93   John 1:13
94   Luke 3:22
95   Acts 2:

The Bride will be willing

Gen. 24:8 'If the woman is unwilling to come back with you, then you will be released from this oath of mine, only do not take my son back there.'

The chosen Bride of Christ is longing to depart this earthly domain and be with her Lord. Sadly, many who profess the name of Jesus are actually unwilling to forsake the things of this world and are quite unprepared to follow the leading of the Holy Spirit. This is an incredibly dangerous position for any person to be in. Without following the Holy Spirit the Bride will get lost and will be unable to find the way on her own. The Holy Spirit is the gentle comforter and he will not force the Bride to go where she refuses to follow. He guides and leads but he does not control or coerce. The Bride of Christ is never pushed into a forced marriage. It may

> *'The Bride of Christ is never pushed into a forced marriage.'*

be an arranged relationship but she is always free to make her own choice in every situation. A genuine believer chooses to follow Jesus and wilfully agrees to belong to him. He may gently persuade them but he will never harshly manipulate them. Jesus desires a Bride who is in full control of her actions and who has given her heart as a gift, not through manipulation and unreasonable demands. He desires a lover and a friend, not a cowering slave.

The Bride must be willing to move. All who follow Jesus have to accept that they are on a journey to be with him. The Holy Spirit is leading them away from this world to the Father's house. All who belong to Christ have set their hearts on pilgrimage and know that they do not belong to this world. They cannot settle on the earth surrounded by corruption and they long for the security and freedom of heaven. Too many Christians are so comfortable on earth that they will not move into what God has for their lives. They behave more like Lot's wife than the Bride of Christ and it seems that even strong angels can't drag them away from their love of the world.[96]

At some stage in life all believers will have to depart and be with Christ and, like Paul, should desire to do so.[97] Christians cannot demand that Jesus accommodate their lifestyle and insist that he lives where they are. The Holy Spirit is not obliged to fit in to someone's church routine or leave people in their religious comfort zones. His role is to change people from their present mind-set and lifestyle and make them like Jesus. He prepares the Bride to be ready for Jesus so that she can go and be with him. When Jesus came he finished all his work on the cross. The Holy Spirit will not bring him back to die again; he expects the church to follow him. Christ is calling his Bride to himself and the Spirit is on a quest to bring her. He has promised the Father he will do it and he is very serious about his mission. Those who are willing to go will be taken and those who stubbornly resist him and refuse will be left behind.

---

96   Gen. 19:16
97   Phil. 1:23

The Bride will be Ready

Gen. 24:13-14 '"I am standing beside this spring and the daughters of the townspeople are coming out to draw water. May it be that when I say to a girl, 'Please let down your jar that I may have a drink,' and she says 'Drink, and I'll water your camels too'- let her be the one you have chosen for your servant Isaac.'"

The Lord always waits by the waters to find his true Bride. Unclean spirits may dwell in waterless places,[98] but the Holy Spirit finds the Bride by the side of clean waters. Moses[99] found his bride by the water and so did Jacob.[100] It was also at a well of water that Jesus revealed his true identity to the Samaritan woman.[101] These women came to satisfy natural thirst, but within them was a deeper thirst that natural water could never quench. This desire is within every soul. All people long for something more than this world can offer, something that satisfies permanently. Nothing in the natural realm can quench that deep spiritual thirst, it is an eternal desire that yearns to be re-connected to the life that Eve lost in the garden. It is the thirst of the true Bride. The Creator understands this longing in the soul of man and watches for those who are sincerely searching, as he waits by the water. He waits and declares that whoever is thirsty can come to him and drink. If they drink they will receive the water of his word, the water of his Spirit and out of their innermost being shall flow the river of living water.[102] It is only the chosen Bride who will listen, understand and take these truths to heart. It is directly through her

---

98	Matt. 12:43
99	Exod. 2:17
100	Gen. 29:10
101	John 4:26
102	John 7:38

actions at the well that she is recognised. Those who desire to belong to him wait at the water and connect with him through his word and through his Spirit. When a person comes to the water, the Spirit sees them and he chooses them because they have also chosen him. When the Bride has correctly positioned herself to connect with God, then the Spirit can do his work and the Bride can be approached. When the Spirit then moves into action upon the church, her real purpose can be revealed and her future destiny can unfold.

5

The Coming Bride

'Without saying a word, the man watched her closely to learn whether
or not the Lord had made his journey successful.'
Gen. 24:21

When reading about the brides in the Bible, it is clear that Eve was created and Sarah was already married, but Rebekah had to be found. Just as the Holy Spirit moved above the waters during creation, He now waits beside waters to connect with the future Bride. He will not take the wrong Bride to the Son; she must be the right one, the perfect one. Although watching and waiting he does not speak at first, the Spirit must observe the correct response – a mustard seed of faith – before he will act. He knows that the future Bride will have specific characteristics and attributes, so a test is set to discover her true identity.

Gen. 24:15-16 'Before he had finished praying, Rebekah came...She was the daughter of Bethuel son of Milcah, who was the wife of Abraham's brother Nahor. The girl was very beautiful, a virgin; no man had ever lain with her.'

Rebekah was from the same family tree as Abraham. The chosen bride must have the same linage as Abraham's son Isaac. Whilst this was an essential criterion of the bride in Genesis, it is also a necessary condition of Christ's future Bride. The Holy Spirit will only choose a Bride who has the same DNA of the Son. She must have faith and she must be born from above. The Spirit only recognises the Bride who is of the same family as Jesus as only those born of God can belong to the true church. She was very beautiful and in the eyes of God the Bride always has an unsurpassed beauty. The church may not be seen as attractive in the eyes of the world, but God looks at the true inward nature of an individual. His Bride has true beauty, not the superficial beauty of outward adornment, but the inner, unfading beauty of a gentle and quite spirit, which is of great worth in God's sight.[103] To the Bridegroom, she is altogether lovely and he always declares this truth to her, 'How beautiful you are, my darling! Oh how beautiful!'[104]

Rebekah was also pure, she did not belong to anyone else and she could not have been used to satisfy another man's desires. Likewise the church belongs to Christ and to him alone. She is espoused as a chaste virgin to him and must not be polluted by the uncleanness of men. The Spirit of God is holy and pure and he looks for the same attributes in his church. Jesus is Holy, so his Bride will be Holy.[105]

---

103   1 Pet. 3:3,4
104   Song of Songs 1:15
105   1 Pet. 1:16

Gen. 24:18-19 "Drink my lord" she said, and she gave him a drink...
"I'll draw water for your camels too, until they have finished drinking."

Many women came out of the town, but only one would pass the test. The passing of the test would be decided upon the condition of her inner attitude: whether the woman possessed a servant heart or if she would only come to the well to satisfy her own thirst. Unfortunately, many professed Christians attend church mainly out of a desire to enjoy the meeting or to attain self-satisfaction. Self-absorbed Christians want their needs to be met, their emotions to be soothed and their intellect to be satisfied. This is not the motivation or behaviour of the true Bride. She is there to satisfy God. Rebekah ensured that the servant at the well was given a drink. Sincere Christians do not primarily focus on whether they like the music or the preaching style because they are there to worship and serve God. It is he who should be satisfied and it is Jesus who must be given a drink.[106]

Rebekah not only served the messenger, she also attended to the camels. This is a real test of a servant bride, and the place where many fail. A lot of people will call Jesus Lord, but will not do what he said.[107] Some Christians draw the line at serving camels because camels are ugly, smell bad, drink a lot and never say thank you. Would Rebekah really keep serving and working away until ten camels were satisfied and had finished drinking? Camels do not show any appreciation no matter how well they are served. This was a lot of hard work and long unpleasant toil for such a beautiful woman to undertake, but she was a woman of noble character

---

106   John 4:7
107   Luke 6:46

and her arms were strong for the task.[108] Without any hint of murmuring
or complaint Rebekah 'ran' to get the water, passing the test without even
knowing it. Her ultimate destiny was being decided even as she humbly
served an unknown stranger. Throughout all of this, the divine marriage
planner was watching her work and he always chooses servant-hearted
women to belong to the Son.

Elijah's widow[109] and Elisha's Shunammite[110] are just two examples out
of many unnamed women who entertained strangers and received God's
blessing as a result. It was the same in the New Testament. Little is known
about women such as Joanna, Susanna 'and many others'[111] who served
and supported Jesus out of their own means. What is certain is that they
were known and chosen by Jesus. It is interesting to note that it was often
the women who were a greater help to
Jesus, rather than the men. Their reward
is certain. God has always been looking
for a servant Bride, one who will go the
extra mile in her duty and care. He is
searching for someone who entertains

*'The Bride must
be the perfect
match for the
groom.'*

strangers and cares for the unattractive, unclean and unappreciative. The
Bride must be the perfect match for the groom. She has to have the same
spirit and attitude as Christ. He was the servant king who came to give his
life in service to others and his partner will have a similar heart to share
in his work.

---

108   Prov. 31:17
109   1 Kings 17:9
110   2 Kings 4:8
111   Luke 8:3

Gen. 24:22 'When the camels had finished drinking, the man took out a gold nose ring...and two gold bracelets.'

Before explaining anything, expensive gifts were given to Rebekah. What was she to make of this, who was this man, what was he giving her and what were his motives? She could not possibly have understood or explained what was happening to her at that moment. These were very valuable gifts, but should she accept them without knowing more details? After the Bride has been correctly identified, the Holy Spirit cannot resist lavishing gifts upon her. When God sees genuine faith and an open heart he responds by pouring out his gifts, just as he did in Cornelius's house.[112] Likewise, when a church enters into a genuine relationship of submission to the Holy Spirit, the giving of his gifts also increases. He loves to bestow his gifts on the Bride of Christ and he has never stopped doing so. His people may not understand everything that is happening at first, just as the early church may not have understood everything about the Spirit's gifts on the day of Pentecost. As the relationship between the Bride and the Spirit deepens and persists, the church will come to understand, like Rebekah, that even greater gifts are to come.

Gen. 24:23 'Then he asked, "Whose daughter are you?"'

The messenger needed to hear a clear declaration from this woman. He could have easily found out who she was from other people, but he wanted to hear her own confession of who she claimed to be. Rebekah didn't respond by stating her own name, but by declaring who she belonged to, 'I am the daughter of Bethuel. Bethuel means 'dweller in God.' The

---

112   Acts 10:44-46

true bride does not boast of her beauty, fame or her own name, but, in humility, she confesses whose name she bears and to whom she belongs. She honours her parents and her people.

In this day of self-promotion when people create their own titles and name their ministries after themselves, a submissive and humble spirit like Rebekah's is often hard to find. A true child of God should have the same confession as Rebekah. They do not love to promote their own name and achievements, but they humbly confess that they belong to God. They state that they are dwellers in God and their home is with him. The Holy Spirit always responds to a true confession and he will uphold the Bride who desires to dwell with God.

Gen. 24:25 'She added, "We have room for you to spend the night."'

Rebekah is kind and offers hospitality to the stranger. She may not have understood everything that was going on, but she wanted the presence of this messenger to abide with her and invited him into her father's house. She could not have anticipated the full consequences of her actions. It would change everything in her life. When someone invites the Holy Spirit into their lives and home they may not initially understand the full implications and consequences of that decision. One thing is certain, however, his presence will change everything. He comes to reveal the divine plan for every believer in the church. He comes to bring supernatural gifts and revelation, but his main objective is that he has come to possess the Bride and to take her to be with the Son, forever. Many churches do not grasp the fullness of his role. Like Rebekah's brother Laban they joyfully accept the Spirit because of his gifts and the wonderful revelation that he brings. They can sometimes see a use for him in their meetings, but God's Spirit is not there to be used. He is on a mission and no one should fail to recognise that he is there to take control of the Bride and to take the Church to be with Jesus. All in the church must listen to what he says, when he gives further revelation of the purpose of his divine mission.

The Spirit Speaks to the Church

Gen. 24: 33 'I will not eat until I have told you what I have to say.'
Rev. 2:7 'He who has an ear, let him hear what the Spirit says to the churches.'

When the messenger enters the household of the bride he recites the conversation that he had with Abraham. He explains his purpose in searching for a bride for Isaac. When the Holy Spirit speaks to the church he repeats the purpose of his mission, which is to identify the true Bride. Just like the servant in the narrative, the Spirit speaks about the Father and about the Son. He always honours the other members of the Trinity. He reveals the desires of the Father and the Son and he takes their glory and makes it known to the church. Those who are listening can hear the Spirit's words, but those that are superficial merely get obsessed with his gifts and power. It is interesting to note that he first speaks to the leaders of the household before speaking to Rebekah. God usually speaks to leaders before the whole church and good pastors listen and are prepared to obey even if it means loss to their own congregation. Carnal leaders, like Laban, may ignore the Holy Spirit's primary role and use the Bride to increase prestige for themselves. Very immature leaders try to manipulate proceedings in order to get the Spirit to perform tricks like Samson in the Philistine temple.[113] Fortunately, Rebekah's leadership wisely allowed her to choose her own destiny.

The Bride is Released

Gen. 24:50-51 'this is from the LORD...Here is Rebekah; take her and go, and let her become the wife of your master's son, as the LORD has directed.

Rebekah's overseers recognised the voice of God and understood that it was futile to oppose the direction of the LORD and the leading of the Holy Spirit. They submitted to the words of the servant and consented to her being taken where he wanted her to be. As soon as they released their control over her, expensive gifts were given to all members of the household. Once a leader submits to God and lays down their control over the church, the Holy Spirit increases his blessing over the house. The whole church increases in blessing and gifts when his will is allowed to be done. Rebekah's leaders were to guide and protect her but never to stop her from being taken for God's plan and purpose. All leaders in God's church must follow the same pattern. The Holy Spirit is very jealous over the Bride and he has chosen her for the purposes of the Father and the Son. No leader should dare to restrict the Spirit when he comes to fulfil the destiny of his church.

---

113   Judges 5:25

Here Am I, Send Me

Gen. 24:58 'they called Rebekah and asked her, "Will you go with this man?" "I will go," she said.'

The messenger made his purpose and mission very clear and the leaders agreed with him and gave their blessing and consent over Rebekah's future. It is very important that anyone starting on a new life or ministry gets someone in spiritual authority to send and bless them. But Rebekah still had to make her own choice. The Bride of Christ must always choose and act out of her own free will and conscience. Her leaders cannot choose for her and the Spirit will not force her, so she has to speak for herself. The true Bride in scripture always makes the choice of faith, just as Ruth chose to leave her people in Moab and go to Bethlehem.[114] The bride in the Song of Songs sums up the declaration on behalf of everyone who belongs to Christ, 'Take me away with you, let us hurry!'[115] This is the true cry of every heart that belongs to Jesus, as they long for his appearing. Everyone must make the choice to either stay where they are, or to move closer to him. The Father and the Son have done everything possible to obtain the Bride. The Spirit is waiting for the response of everyone who is called and the only decision that still remains is whether they go with him. The journey may be long and the approaching camel ride could be uncomfortable, but if the Bride perseveres under the guidance of the Spirit, he will take her to Jesus and his mission will not fail.

---

114   Ruth 1:16
115   Song of Songs 1:4

The Bride and Groom see each other

Gen. 24:63-64 'As Isaac looked up he saw camels approaching. Rebekah also looked up and saw Isaac.'

Isaac saw Rebekah first. Just like Nathanael under the fig tree,[116] Jesus always sees someone before they first see him. He is the God who particularly watches over the needy woman.[117] He gazes at his coming bride even while she is a long way off. He sees the camels and all the discomfort that it represents. He knows the journey has been long and he understands that his coming bride has lost so much of the life that she once knew. He is aware that she may still have many fears, but he knows that she is in the safe hands of the Comforter and Counsellor. He recognises her straight away because she is wearing the clothes that he sent to her. The bride has made herself ready and he is coming out to meet her. She does not recognise him at first, just as Jesus was not recognised even by his own disciples,[118] but the faithful guide at her side speaks gently and clearly, 'It is the Master'. The coming Bride has finally arrived. They meet each other and Isaac, the son, immediately takes his bride into the dwelling that is already prepared for her.

Married

Gen. 24:67 'He married Rebekah. So she became his wife, and he loved her.'

The plan had worked: father Abraham was happy, the messenger was successful and the son was satisfied. Isaac had obtained his bride. The

---

116   John 1:48
117   Gen. 16:13
118   Luke 24:16

promises of God would now be fulfilled. Israel would be born, the Messiah would come, and mankind could be saved. Just as this was true in the Genesis story, so it will take place in God's greater purpose for the Bride. The future Bride of Christ will also come to Jesus the Son, the Spirit will not fail, and the Father's desire will 'be done on earth as it is in heaven.'[119]

The divine narrative then says that Isaac 'loved her.' Jesus loves his Bride also, which is so simple yet profound beyond comprehension. No greater love has ever been known than the love that God had for mankind. 'For God so loved the world'[120] is the greatest statement ever made. Jesus loves you, and he proved it at the cross. Isaac never had eyes for any other woman. Unlike so many other men in the Old Testament he never desired more than one bride and never loved another woman. Rebekah was everything to him; he loved her and her alone, just as Christ loves his church.

---

119   Matt. 6:10
120   John 3:16

6

Battle of the Brides

'Laban had two daughters; the name of the older was Leah, and the
name of the younger was Rachel.'
Gen. 29:16

*J*acob needed to find his bride, just like his father Isaac had before him. His parents had told him where to go to find her and from which family she would come. Jacob obeyed, went to the right place and found the correct family. The problem was that there was more than one woman who fulfilled the necessary requirements. His dilemma was in making the right decision and ensuring that he worked to obtain the right wife. Jacob thought that he had made the right choice and given the required sacrifice of service, but things would not turn out the way he had planned. God had other plans and despite Jacob's intentions both Rachel and Leah would become legitimate brides of Israel. Man's plans for the Bride are not always God's plans. The next brides of Israel would be very different from each other but still accepted by God. They can serve to illustrate two different styles of church or types of characteristics found amongst God's people. Given the choice between Rachel and Leah, it is interesting to observe which type of church most people would choose.

Outward or Inner Beauty?

Gen. 29:17 'Leah had weak eyes, but Rachel was lovely in form, and beautiful.'

Naturally speaking, Jacob was going to choose the best looking bride. In appearance, Rachel possessed everything a man would desire. She was young, had good eyes and had a lovely shape. Leah, on the other hand, was just not his type. Many people view Christ's Bride in a similar way. They look at her from the outward appearance and, in doing so, assess God's church based on faulty assumptions.

Firstly, Rachel looked great. Carnal men assess women primarily upon their appearance and carnal Christians often choose their church in the same way. They want their church to look good and sadly that is their first and sometimes only consideration. The form of Rachel looked better than other women's and was more appealing to Jacob's needs. The services of some churches can sometimes be so focused in appealing to the natural senses that they almost ignore the requirements of God altogether. They assume that people could not possibly attend an unfashionable church meeting in a poorly decorated building without fancy lights or state-of-the-art decorations. What would their friends think of them if they belonged to an ugly church? Of course, this is a foolish way of viewing the church, as every student of the Bible knows the outward promotion and appearance of an individual rarely has any real connection with their future fruitfulness. 'Man looks at the outward appearance, but the LORD looks at the heart.'[121] His church should be viewed in the same way. Rachel may have attracted a larger crowd of boys hanging around her because of her beauty, but Leah would birth more men of God. Leah my not have looked as good as Rachel but she would bear the most children by far.

Secondly, Rachel was younger than Leah, maybe considerably younger. Who wants to marry a thirty year old if you can have a twenty year old? The obsession with youth is not a modern phenomenon. Youth is often chosen over age and experience, as young people are usually more naïve and easier to control than wiser, more mature people. This was a terrible error of judgement on Jacob's part, as Rachel, despite being the youngest, would die before Leah did. Leah would be around to look after the family long after Rachel had passed away. In a similar way, younger, trendier churches can often pass away very quickly, whereas older and more stable ones are more likely to be around for a longer time. God seeks longevity and maturity in his church and good fruit is not always the fastest to grow. When assessing the church as a whole, people should take a long-term view.

Thirdly, Rachel appeared to have better vision that Leah, however, this may not have been the case. In the present world of multiple vision statements, people are often deceived into thinking that because a church talks a lot about vision it must mean that it genuinely has it. Unfortunately, just because something is written on a church wall does not mean it will come to pass or that it is even from God. The vision ability of a church

---

121   1 Sam. 16:7

is one of the most talked about attributes in today's Christian world with some leaders talking more about their vision than they do about Christ. The vision of the church should be continually refocusing to see Christ most clearly. Great people in the Bible always wanted to see more of Jesus. A Pastor's main role is to prepare the Bride to see her Bridegroom and to give the church a clearer vision of Jesus. What a person continually looks at is

> *'if the Bride is consistently gazing at other things, then she may end up becoming an unfaithful church.'*

often what they most desire, as Eve learnt to her detriment.[122] If the Bride is constantly gazing at other things, then she may end up becoming an unfaithful church. Rachel looked good and she knew it. But Leah sought to satisfy her husband. People must not be deceived about a church's claim to have great vision, as it is not about how it looks but about who it is looking at. The faithful Bride is always gazing at the one her heart loves, Jesus.

I'm in the Wrong Church!

Gen. 29:25 'When morning came, there was Leah! So Jacob said to Laban, "What is this you have done to me? I served you for Rachel, didn't I?"

After seven years of faithful service, Jacob woke up one morning and discovered that he was married to the wrong woman. This was not what he had planned and not what he had worked so hard for. He felt shocked

---

122   Gen. 3:6

and betrayed, but God was still in control of deciding the purpose and the future of the bride. Although he felt disappointed, deceived and confused the truth was much deeper than he grasped. He was given the bride that the father had chosen, not the one his flesh desired. If only Christians – especially leaders – would take this principle to heart. No one should belong to the church that you desire, but should be given to the one that the Father chooses.

Despite his misgivings, Jacob did not in fact have the wrong wife; he had been given the exact bride that God had pre-destined for him all along. God knew that it was only through Leah that some of the mightiest saints in the Bible would come. All servants of God need to ask themselves whether they are serving God for the church that they want and only ministering to get the church that satisfies their own desires. Just like Jacob, everyone must genuinely face and deal with this very real issue. What do people do when things don't turn out as they planned and they realise that church has not developed the way they wanted? Their response should be to ask the Father what has happened and they may discover that God intended it that way. It may have been his plan all along, so that his Bride would turn out exactly the way he had ordained it. Fortunately, Jacob would not leave in anger, issue a divorce or shun Leah. He would also marry Rachel and continue to faithfully work for his brides with the result being increase and fruitfulness for the whole family. God loves all members of his church and everyone who understands the full nature of the Bride of Christ will have a similar attitude.

The Unloved Bride

Gen. 29:31 'When the LORD saw that Leah was not loved, he opened her womb, but Rachel was barren.'

Leah was fully aware that she was not loved as much as Rachel. The Genesis narrative reveals this very clearly. Leah attempted to earn Jacobs love through her efforts at bearing children. When her first-born arrived she declared that, 'surely my husband will love me now.'[123] It did not work, so she doubled her efforts and tried even harder. By child number three she thought, 'now at last my husband will become attached to me, because I have borne him three sons.'[124] However, working to achieve someone's acceptance is futile, as true love cannot be earned. Real love is not conditional. Love is the gift God gives to everyone and he 'demonstrates his own love for us in this: while we were still sinners, Christ died for us.'[125] The fact is that Leah was loved more than she could ever know, not by her natural husband, but by her spiritual one. God's love for his Bride is already complete and perfect. The church never earned love from God; it was his gift to her in Jesus Christ.

God saw that Leah was not loved and when he sees a love vacuum in someone's life he longs to fill it. 'The earth trembles when a married woman is unloved'[126] as God's creation cannot bear a marriage relationship without love. Jesus will always ensure that his Bride knows that she is loved and Leah would come to realise this by the birth of her fourth son. By the time Judah was born, several years of an unhappy marriage had

---

123   Gen. 29:32.
124   Gen. 29:34
125   Rom. 5:8
126   Prov. 30:21-23.

gone by and she had learned to 'praise the Lord.'[127] When people praise God for who he is instead of trying to earn favour through achievements, they have started to live by grace and not works.[128] Everyone must come to the position where they rejoice in God's love for them, not in their abilities to please him or others. It is by grace that God's Bride has been saved; and it is through the gift of faith, given by God, not by works. When Leah arrived at this revelation, God had obtained the Bride he was looking for. When she praised God at the birth of Judah the ultimate expression of love could come to the earth, as it was from his loins that Jesus Christ – 'the lion of the tribe of Judah[129]' – would come. Through the faithfulness of Leah, all nations on earth are now blessed with true love. No member of Christ's Bride is unloved, but Leah's love was not found in this world, it came from her heavenly Bridegroom.

Outward Success at any Cost

Gen. 30:1 'Give me children or I'll die!'

Rachel may have looked beautiful and might have received all the attention from people, but it was Leah that would receive the most blessing from God. As time went by, Rachel came to understand that looking good was not as important as it seemed. She was still barren. No church can bear the stigma of barrenness forever no matter how good they look on the outside and, ultimately, they must do something about it. Rachel did what countless churches have tried to do and failed. She tried to produce fruit by illegitimate methods and followed Sarah's folly of using her

---

127   Gen. 29:30
128   Eph. 2:8,9
129   Rev. 5:5

maidservant to produce children. Although God always planned to use Rachel and intended to make her fruitful, she was not prepared to wait any longer. Churches today repeat the same mistakes of their forbears and end up reproducing the same pain and trouble as a consequence.

Rachel started her campaign by playing the blame game. She believed that it was Jacob who was not giving her children and decided she would not put up with it. The same attitude is seen in so many Christians today. People feel unfruitful and unfulfilled, so they blame someone – usually one of their leaders – for their lack of fulfilment, instead of seeing that it may be God leading them to a stronger faith. Rachel failed to acknowledge that Jacob was enabling others to become pregnant, so perhaps the problem was with her. Ignoring Jacob's advice that God was in control, Rachel decided that she would force something to happen. She unfortunately believed that birthing anything was better than being barren – why use faith in God when you can engineer success with your own resourcefulness? And so the servant girl was summoned, ignoring the failed experiment between Sarah and Hagar a couple of generations before.

Bilhah was promptly impregnated and the folly of Jacob's grandparents was repeated. The result was Dan, who became head of the most unfaithful tribe in the history of Israel. Dan was a tribe who deserted its inheritance, set up a false priesthood and worshipped calf idols. Even Samson – Dan's most gifted leader – was a moral failure. Samson himself never treated the women in his life with proper respect and honour. How a minister treats their spouse is a strong indication of how they will treat the church.

He failed to protect his original bride,[130] used prostitutes[131] and ended up being destroyed by a deceitful and unfaithful woman.[132] He would come to epitomise everything that is wrong with church leadership: charismatic and gifted, but a failure when recognising the importance of the Bride. Samson had a strong public gifting, but it was coupled with severe character faults and sinful habits that would eventually leave him a blind prisoner being mocked by God's enemies.

The whole family would suffer the consequences of Rachel's actions. Because Jacob used Bilhah, she would later suffer abuse at the hands of one of his sons.[133] Once a bad example has been set it is sadly copied by the next generation.

Many Churches of today follow Rachel's folly. They assume that any method of ministry offering quick results will be approved by God, but he never intended to impregnate slave women. He desires free children birthed out of the love covenant that he has with his free Bride. However, many churches commit the same errors of Rachel, and birth Dan instead of Judah. The ultimate result is a legacy like Dan's: failure in ministry, a corrupt priesthood, visionless leadership, moral bankruptcy, abandoned inheritance and false worship. And once this false system of success has been started, it is hard to stop. In the battle between the brides, children are born to maidservants and even Leah ends up copying Rachel's misguided methods to obtain further fruitfulness. In other words, when the church down the road has a gimmick that seems to work, it will not

---

130   Judges 15:6
131   Judges 16:1
132   Judges 16:4
133   Gen. 35:22

be long before every church in town is copying it. Many Churches copy methods without thinking about whether it has God's approval, as they reason that, 'if it works in one church, it must be good'. This faulty logic can birth big problems. It bypasses the revelation that God's primary interest is in his Bride being fruitful, not a system of production and multiplication by means of slavery.

Church Rivalry

Gen. 30:8 'Rachel said, "I have had a great struggle with my sister, and I have won."'

The Levitical law prohibiting a man from marrying his wife's sister had not yet been implemented.[134] This law predicted that such sisters would become rivals and Rachel and Leah became embroiled in a bitter struggle to see which bride would be the best. It was an unpleasant conflict and caused real pain to all involved. Rachel knew she was ahead in the beauty competition, but Leah was winning in production and output. The battle intensified and became increasingly bitter with each bride fighting to win. If observed rationally, the situation can be seen for the foolishness that it is. They should not have been in competition as they were both equally the bride of Jacob and members of the same household. They would both become great women in God's history book and they would both bear children that would be blessed by God. Rachel did not know it at the time, but she would birth Joseph one of the most perfect people in scripture. However, they were so engrossed in their petty little dispute that they lost sight of the bigger picture and God's ultimate aim.

---

134   Lev. 18:18

As foolish as the rivalry in this story is, many Christians and churches are currently engaged in similar battles. It is seldom acknowledged publically, but these conflicts are present nevertheless. Churches can often be seen trying to prove that they look more attractive and have better fruit than other congregations. Leaders can sometimes be caught trying to out-do other pastors in the unspoken ministry success competition. Rachel said that Leah had lost the struggle and that she had won. But won what? There was never any competition as far as the heavenly Bridegroom was concerned. According to his assessment of the situation they were both victorious because they were both the Bride. Ultimately, people must see the church the way Jesus views it. If not, lives and ministries may descend into pointless comparison with others that will only produce bitterness. Paul said, 'If you keep on biting and devouring each other, watch out or you will be destroyed by each other.'[135] All of God's people are victorious through the battle that Christ fought for them. The Bride in Christ shares all things and she is already more than a conqueror through him who loved her.[136]

Hopefully, Rachel and Leah came to some kind of reconciliation in the end. Christ demands unity in his true Bride. Rachel and Leah needed each other more than they would ever know. Rachel's son Joseph would be the one to save all Leah's children from extinction when famine came.[137] Centuries later when Leah's children were massacred in Bethlehem, Rachel would weep as if they were her own.[138] There is only one family

---

135   Gal. 5:15
136   Rom. 8:37
137   Gen. 50:19-21
138   Matt. 2:18

from God's point of view. Any battle between the brides must cease in order for Christ to obtain the church he desires. His church consists of a much wider variety of brides than many have anticipated.

7

The Gentile Bride

'The people of Israel, including the priests and the Levites, have not
kept themselves separate from the neighbouring peoples with their
detestable practices, like those of the Canaanites, Hittites, Perizzites,
Jebusites, Ammonites, Moabites, Egyptians and Amorites. They have
taken some of their daughters as wives for themselves and their sons,
and have mingled the holy race with the peoples around them.'

Ezra 9:1-2

'Do not intermarry with them. Do not give your daughters to their sons
or take their daughters for your sons.'

Deut. 7:3

After the brides of the Patriarchs had birthed their children, the
embryonic nation of Israel had arrived. Abraham, Isaac and Jacob had
come to understand that God's emphasis was on making the bride fruitful
and that she must be pure 'because he was seeking Godly offspring' for

himself.[139] These brides had all been obtained from the same extended family, sharing similar DNA. Having established the prerequisite holiness of the Bride, God's word reinforced the understanding and importance of this purity. To achieve this he identified specific people groups that served as examples of uncleanliness in his sight, which his nation were not to intermarry with. God listed these specific gentile nations and stated that their women could not be married to his people. These gentile tribes, because of their various unclean practices, were excluded from union with himself and his holy nation.

He made it very clear what the rules were by writing them down in several places, to ensure that the Jewish nation understood. After laying down these laws, God did something unthinkable. Throughout the Bible we observe God appearing to allow people to break his own laws regarding marriage. In doing so he reveals another law greater than the written code: the law of love. This higher law reveals another mystery of the Bride that God is preparing for himself. As shall be seen, God specifically and purposefully pre-ordains brides from each of the above prohibited tribes and includes them in his nation's genealogy.

'They do not inherit the holy DNA from their ancestors, but obtain purity from their bridegroom through marriage.'

These woman, although originally from excluded gentile nations, are essential to God's outworking of his divine plan. They do not inherit the holy DNA from their ancestors, but obtain purity from

---

139   Mal. 2:15

their bridegroom through marriage. They represent the gentile bride that is coming to Christ and the church that God loves.

The Canaanite brides

Gen. 28:1 'Isaac called for Jacob...and commanded him, "Do not marry a Canaanite woman."'

Gen. 38:2 'Judah met the daughter of a Canaanite man...he married her and lay with her.'

Even before Jacob had passed from this world, his sons were ignoring his example and taking wives from the forbidden tribes. Judah began the practice of marrying excluded women and his decedents continued this habit throughout the generations. Of all Israel's tribes, it should have been Judah that remained pure. It was the tribe of the king, the line of David, the genealogy of Messiah and should have stayed untainted from gentile seed. But here is seen the great mystery hidden away in God's word. 'This mystery is that through the gospel the Gentiles are heirs together with Israel, members together of one body.'[140] Just as Judah took a Canaanite wife, so his greatest ancestor Jesus Christ would also take a gentile church as his Bride. Jesus provided an example, when the Canaanite woman knelt at his feet and he would not listen to the complaints of those around him to send her away. When she knelt and in faith confessed Jesus as Lord, he gave her what she requested.[141] God still accepts gentile believers to belong to him, even if they originally came from one of the prohibited nations.

---

140   Eph. 3:6
141   Matt. 15:22-28

Tamar and Rahab were both Canaanites. They would not have been the first choice of women to be called to ultimately bear some of the greatest kings that walked the earth. There is no doubt, however, that they are a picture of the true Bride of Christ, as they both appear in his genealogical line.[142] Despite their future prestige, their entire tribe were originally born under a curse, as it says, 'cursed be Canaan! The lowest of slaves will he be.' [143]

It was not only the Canaanites who were born under a curse; all children of Adam and Eve were born under the same curse as their parents. Humanity's rebellious nature was present even at birth. Born into the family of fallen mankind, no one had any legitimate claim to share in the blessings of God any more than Adam and Eve had access to the tree of life. Living under mankind's curse would result in death and eternal separation from God for every living soul. No one born into this world can confidently entertain any prospect of earthly blessing, because everyone has inherited a sinful nature from their ancestors. This was specifically the case of all Canaanites, as they inherited even greater curses. Despite the presence of this curse overshadowing their lives, Tamar and Rahab would come to experience another nature and life that would cancel out their Canaanite curse. This power would come through the blessed nature of Judah, the bloodline of the King and DNA of Jesus Christ. The seed of Judah would enter these women, they would receive his life and they would become his bride. In a spiritual sense this astonishing fact is also true of all members of God's church. When the life of Jesus enters a

---

142   Matt. 1:3-5
143   Gen. 9:25

person, no matter what their ancestral background their curse is removed and they are blessed along with everyone chosen to belong to him. The curse of the old nature cannot overcome the power of the new life that comes from the bridegroom who blesses his people. The inherited consequences of sin and death are overcome by the head of the church, Jesus Christ. His Bride receives a new life, her curse is reversed and she becomes a new creation blessed by God.

Prostitutes?

Gen. 38:24 'Judah was told, "Tamar is guilty of prostitution.'
Joshua 3:25 'Joshua spared Rahab the prostitute.'

Tamar and Rahab were called prostitutes. Being Canaanites was bad enough, but they also resorted to the immoral profession of prostitution. Instead of focusing on their sins, however, God sees their faith and so 'by faith the prostitute Rahab…was not killed.'[144] It is through their faith that these women reveal the true nature of God's church and, despite sins in their previous life, they become brides saved by faith.

Being prostitutes, both women were used by men but never loved by men. Prostitutes don't experience true love; they endure physical abuse disguised as love. Rahab's clients were only seeking selfish satisfaction by using her body to fulfil their own lusts; they did not love her. Tamar suffered similar abuse from members of her own family. Her dead husband's brother should have fulfilled his duty in making her fruitful,[145] but instead he just used her body to satisfy his flesh.[146] Unfortunately, the

---

144   Heb. 11:31
145   Deut. 25:5-6
146   Gen. 38:8-10

Body of Christ can also be used for carnal purposes today. People often use the church to satisfy their own desires, even being encouraged to 'find the church that gives them what they want.' The purity and devotion of a loving relationship is abandoned in exchange for personal gratification. No woman, especially God's church, should be treated in this way. She is God's holy Bride, not man's handy prostitute. Jesus saved his Bride from this kind of lustful abuse by giving her the true love that she requires and Rahab is a picture of this relationship between Christ and his church. She would finally find a man who truly loved her and would make her fruitful. Both Tamar and Rahab would become fruitful, not through the lusts of men, but by their faith in God. Jesus never uses his Bride to satisfy his desires . He serves her, loves her and fulfils her by making her fruitful. When both of these women married into the tribe of Judah, they were no longer prostitutes – regardless of their previous conduct – but brides, and part of the family of Judah. Both Tamar and Rahab are found listed in the genealogy of Jesus Christ in Matthew's gospel.[147] Despite their original exclusion from God's family their names are now written down in his book, along with everyone who belongs to him by faith.

Asenath The Egyptian

Gen. 41:45 'Pharoah gave Joseph... Asenath the daughter of Potiphera, priest of On, to be his wife.'

How could Asenath belong to God? Every detail that we have about her life reveals that she should be excluded by Israel and not accepted by God.

---

147   Matt. 1:3-5

Asenath was an Egyptian and the people of Israel were not meant to mingle with them, as they represented the land of slavery and everything that they were warned to avoid. Egypt is always a picture of the world in the Bible. It is the place people are told not to love, and the nation believers are called out of and where they will be delivered from. Whenever God's people turned their hearts towards Egypt, God was not pleased. How could Joseph, the most favoured child of Jacob, be married to an Egyptian? It is because she represents the Bride – the church – and despite originally belonging to this world, she was now delivered from it through marriage to her bridegroom. Just as Asenath could never have found a greater husband than Joseph, every believer has found their deliverance through a perfect Bridegroom, Israel's ultimate son Jesus Christ. Jesus said that his people were 'not of the world, even as I am not of it.'[148] Whatever her original nationality, even one being completely of this world, the Bride now belongs to heaven.

Gen. 41:50 'The daughter of Potiphera, priest of On.'
Asenath appeared to have a bigger problem than her nationality prohibiting her from God's presence. Each of the three times she is mentioned in the book of Genesis she is also called 'the daughter of Potiphera, priest of On.' Some authorities translate her name as 'belonging to the Goddess Neith,' and others as 'belonging to father.' When considering that her father was Potiphera the Priest of On who was a sun worshipper, it can be inferred that her life had been surrounded by the worship of false gods. Being from an Egyptian priestly family, Asenath was accustomed

---

148   John 17:16

to having many different gods in her life. She knew lots of false gods, but she knew nothing of the real one. When she became the bride of Joseph all of this would have to change. In order to be the bride of Joseph she would have to accept that there was only one true and living God. No other God could be set before him, as he alone was supreme in Joseph's life. The life of her new husband would have to become a living reality within her life; a mere affirmation to the existence of the real God would not be accepted. So it is with everyone who chooses to belong to Jesus. They cannot claim to leave Egypt but still hope to keep their addictions to the gods of this world. The gods of selfish fame, celebrity status, luxury, greed, idleness, pride, envy and competition all have to be left behind. These gods have no place in the presence of the Lord. Once married, Aseneth no longer belonged to her earthly father who worshipped false gods, but instead she belonged to her husband who worshipped the Lord. In the same way the church receives not only a new husband, but also a new father, 'the God and Father of our Lord Jesus Christ.'[149]

Gen. 46:20 'In Egypt, Manasseh and Ephraim were born to Joseph by Asenath, daughter of Potiphera priest of On.'
Upon Marriage to Joseph Asenath would become fruitful, as God's chosen Bride is always fruitful. She would bear children for her new husband, but they would not be Egyptians they would be children of Israel. Although officially grandchildren to Israel, Jacob would adopt them as his very own sons and they would receive equal inheritance with the other tribes. Asenath's sons Ephraim and Manasseh would come to

---

149   Rom. 15:6

embody the very essence of the nation of Israel. The father agreed to bless and own her children because she was married to his favourite son who was also the saviour of Egypt. The children of God are accepted by the Father for the same reason today. They may have a past history of false worship and of belonging to the world, but now that they belong to God's beloved Son, the saviour of the world, he adopts them as his own. The Church, along with all its true members, are blessed and receive a full inheritance from God.

Ruth the Moabite Woman.

Neh. 13:1 'No Moabite should ever be admitted into the assembly of God.'

Ruth came from a special class of unclean people, the Moabites. Moab's parents originated from Sodom and were birthed through incest and accustomed to sexual perversion.[150] This sexual sin continued through the generations so that by the time of Moses it was connected with false worship and God had to punish Israel for committing indecent sexual acts with Moabite women.[151] The Moabites, especially the women, were specifically identified as indulging in sinful practices and were excluded from God's presence as a result. Despite all of this, Ruth was chosen from amongst the Moabites to be a bride that belonged to God.

Today God still chooses people to belong to him despite their background of horrendous sins. Some people can be misled into believing that some sins are just too bad for God to forgive. Some feel that their background

---

150   Gen. 19:36
151   Num.25:1-5

is just too perverted for them to be accepted. Even when some people do have faith in God, they can still feel a burden of shame and guilt over their former lifestyle. Ruth may have felt some of this, but she overcame the uncleanliness of her ancestry to such an extent that she was declared 'a woman of noble character.'[152] Ruth is a wonderful picture of the true Bride of Christ.

Ruth 4:10 'Ruth, the Moabitess, Mahlon's widow'
Ruth's first marriage was not successful. Perhaps she thought that marrying an Israelite may improve her fortunes, but Mahlon passed away leaving Ruth a widow. Little is recorded of Mahlon's life, but the fragments given are illuminating. Firstly his name means 'sickly' and his brother, Killion meant 'weakling.' Secondly, both men appear to have abandoned the LORD's inheritance in Bethlehem to live outside the land of promise.[153] If their example was a true representation of the average Israelite's character, then Ruth didn't have a very positive introduction to the nature and identity of their God. The LORD of Israel was neither weak nor sick and he never intended his people to be either. She could easily have been discouraged and depressed at the failure and loss of the men in her life and, like many people today, could have resorted to blaming God for her predicament. Fortunately, she saw something noble in the character of her mother in law Naomi and this most likely attracted her attention towards the God of Abraham, Isaac and Jacob. The positive consequences of Ruth seeing something good in Naomi resulted in her

---

152   Ruth 3:11
153   Ruth 1:1-2

famous declaration of faith, 'Your people will be my people and your God my God.'[154]

It is often the case that the best reflection of a man is seen in his bride, just as God said 'Woman is the glory of man.'[155] Ruth saw something of God's glory in Naomi and chose to stay with her. Through her connection to Naomi, this gentile bride came to know God through the faith of this Israelite woman. Some can see in this relationship a picture of the church coming to share in the promise that God gave to the Jews. Whilst this may be true, it is also correct that when looking at the church unbelievers should glimpse the glory of Christ.[156] Through this simple faith they, like Ruth, will have an opportunity to connect with him as their redeemer.

Boaz the Bride's Redeemer

Ruth 4:10 'I have acquired Ruth the Moabitess, Mahlon's widow as my wife.'

Upon arriving in the Promised Land Ruth 'set about her work vigorously'[157], as did all women of noble character. Despite being an unclean foreigner and a widow, someone was watching her from a distance. Her deeds were being observed by someone who owned the field in which she worked. This man was Boaz, the 'strong one,'[158] her eventual redeemer and husband. Today many of God's children find themselves in a similar position as Ruth. She was alone, working hard to provide for her family despite being unsure of the future and simply hoping in God. Some

---

154   Ruth 1:16
155   1 Cor. 11:7
156   Eph. 3:21
157   Prov. 31:17
158   Boaz means 'strong'

people are like Ruth now, working in hostile fields amongst strangers who display prejudice towards them. They fear about how they will survive and abandon any hope of a successful and prosperous future.

Just as with Ruth, it is also true that someone is watching and observing every activity of the Bride today. Not sick and weak husbands like the failures of the past, but one who is very strong. He is the one who is willing to be the future redeemer of the Bride. No child of God need ever succumb to the worries of this world or the anxieties of life. Just like Ruth and others who went before, they can know that their 'redeemer lives'[159] and he is going to step in at just the right moment and save them from the barrenness of their situation. Boaz knew all about Ruth, just as Christ knows all about his Bride. He knew all about her background, work and faithfulness. Just as Boaz obtained Ruth at great cost, Jesus also paid the full cost to purchase his Bride and redeem her from her hopeless situation. He longs to cover her with the edge of his garment so that she will belong to him.

Once belonging to Boaz, Ruth would no longer be called an unclean Moabite. She would instead, become known as a bride of the tribe of Judah and would own the field that she once worked in as a servant. Ruth would birth a son, then become the grandmother of Jesse, the father of King David, the man after God's own heart. Both Ruth and Naomi would have a son, and Israel and the gentiles rejoiced together as they would both be saved. God's Bride, despite once being a widow, was now fruitful, as it says 'He settles the childless woman in her home as a happy

---

159   Job 19:25

mother of children.'[160] Just as Ruth was treated by Boaz, so the church is saved and blessed by her heavenly redeemer, Jesus Christ.

Bathsheba of the Hittites

2 Sam. 11:3 'She is Bathsheba...the wife of Uriah the Hittite.'

Like many young women throughout history, Bathsheba must have grown up hoping that she would one day find the man of her dreams. Coming from a good Hebrew family and living near the King's palace in Jerusalem, she may have entertained hopes of someday marrying one of the royal princes of Judah. Instead the unthinkable happened to her, she was married off to a Hittite, a clan of the despised Canaanites.[161] Her hopes must have been dashed that she now belonged to a tribe that her own people did not even believe had a right to live in the Promised Land. Her future looked bleak and unfulfilled with the prospect of no godly inheritance for her children. She may have been born an Israelite, but she now belonged to the unclean gentiles. Any future offspring may not even be acknowledged as true Israelites in the eyes of some people, but may be referred to as despised Hittites. It is almost certain that she could have seen no way out of this predicament, all she could have done was hope in God.

Like Bathsheba, so many people soon discover that their life has not turned out the way they had hoped. They may find themselves in relationships that have no future and in situations that do not look prosperous for them or their families. From a natural understanding they may see no way

---

160   Psalm 133:9
161   Gen. 10:15

out of their situation and it appears almost hopeless to believe that their former dreams could possibly be fulfilled. For people living in this type of circumstance the story of Bathsheba can offer great hope. All who have faith and are called to belong to the King of Israel must never lose hope. As another bride of Judah was once told, 'nothing is impossible with God.'[162] Whatever the cost to the King, he will save the bride that looks to him.

2 Sam. 11:2 'David saw her,' 2 Sam. 11:3 'David enquired about her,'
2 Sam. 11:4 'David took her.'

Bathsheba's beauty had not gone unnoticed. Every Christian should also know that 'the king is enthralled by your beauty.'[163] This future bride was being watched by the eyes of the king even though she already belonged to another. Christ also loved his people while they still belonged to this world, before they were his. Even now he gazes at his church knowing that she will be his future Bride. Whilst the story of Bathsheba and David gets very complicated involving sins of immorality and duplicity, the outcome of the affair can be viewed more favourably in hindsight. Instead of concentrating on the imperfections of fallen people, the prophetic revelation displaying the love that Christ has for his church should be the focus. God always knows the beginning from the end. He had seen her before she knew him, and David would get to know Bathsheba, and take her as his bride.

The consequences of taking Bathsheba would be personally catastrophic

---

162   Luke 1:37
163   Psalm 45:11

for David, but he was willing to pay the price to have the bride he wanted. The penalty of sin is always death. In taking Bathsheba, another man's wife, David would now take upon himself the consequences of this sin that would cost him much pain and suffering. David would pay the price for obtaining this bride. Despite the penalty and bereavement that David would suffer, God's grace would ultimately be given to Bathsheba. Whilst individual sin is never justified by God, he always 'works for the good of those who love him.'[164] The final result, through the grace of God, was that Bathsheba would become the royal bride, birth the future king and be counted in the lineage of Jesus Christ.

Is The Bride a Pawn in Men's Hands?

When reading the story of Bathsheba, it is easy to form the impression that she had little influence in the strong powers affecting and controlling her life. Just like other brides of the Bible, such as Esther,[165] she appears to be caught in a power struggle between the king and other influential men. The Bride can often be seen as a pawn in the hands of the powerful rulers of this world. The lives of the brides in scripture often reveal this important parallel that can be seen in the lives of believers today. God's people can often feel that they have little say over the powerful influences dominating their lives. They can feel that they are being used by those in leadership – religious as well as secular – and have little say in the future direction of their lives. How could this young girl have dared say no to David, God's anointed King? She may have been terrified in his presence

---

164   Rom. 8:28
165   Esther 2:8

to the point of paralysis. She may have been utterly confused by the whole situation so that she no longer grasped whether her actions were right or wrong. She may have reasoned, as many accepted unconditionally, that King David would never do something sinful to anyone. After all, he was a man after God's own heart.

Whatever the real understanding of the situation was in Bathsheba's heart, it can be acknowledged that many today find themselves in similarly perplexing situations. Christians may not always understand the true motives of some leaders in using them the way they do and they can sometimes feel that they are being used primarily out of a leader's desire to exert control over them. Unfortunately, this is all too often the experience of many people in the church today, but God can make everything turn out well for those who trust in him. Bathsheba would be unfairly treated and suffer accusation, loss and bereavement as a result of her relationship with David. Her old husband would die and her firstborn child would not live long.[166] Her feelings of mourning and pain may have been compounded by the belief that she had only submitted to those in authority. Being passively led into sin by those that she trusted would have wounded her deeply. If her trusted leaders had failed her and used her in this way, who could she trust in future? Even in the midst of similar life experiences and feeling of powerlessness, believers can trust in the Lord. If they find themselves being manipulated by imperfect leaders, who use them for their own purposes, the Bride of Christ still knows that good will prevail for those who have faith in God and are called

---

166   2 Sam. 12:15

according to his purposes.[167] Bathsheba's faith in God would still bring her through this difficult trial and his promise for her life would come to fruition.

Royal Bride

2 Sam. 12:24 'Then David comforted his wife Bathsheba, and he went to her and lay with her. She gave birth to son, and they named him Solomon. The LORD loved him.'

Bathsheba's old life came to an end. She had learned that the wages of sin is always death,[168] but her past, despite being painful, was gone and her new life and position would bring blessing from the Lord. God had brought good out of bad. Bathsheba no longer belonged to the Hittites, but was now possessed by the tribe of Judah. In same way the Church of Christ no longer belongs to this world, but she belongs to heaven.

And now she was the royal bride of the king, regardless of her sordid relationships of the past. The Church is also the legal royal Bride of Christ purchased and ratified by his blood. She is no concubine or casual partner, but his wife. As a consequence of this new life, Bathsheba would now birth children and her son, king Solomon, would be born. Unlike her previous offspring of immorality, her next child would be loved by God. So it is with the church. All things birthed by Jesus through his Bride will be loved and owned by God and the life of Jesus will continue to increase through his people. Solomon, the son of Bathsheba, would become the next King through whose wisdom God would bless all mankind.

---

167   Rom. 8:28
168   Rom. 6:23

Naamah the Ammonite

2 Chron. 12:13 'King Rehoboam's mother's name was Naamah; she was an Ammonite.'

Few people have heard of Naamah, but she is essential in understanding the story of the Bride. She was the woman chosen by Solomon to birth the future king, and ultimately, Jesus Christ. Little is known about her other than that 'she was an Ammonite.' Why would Solomon pick Naamah? His choices of bride to pass on the holy DNA were not limited, as he had almost a thousand to choose from![169] Surely he could have chosen someone better than an Ammonite? It seems shocking to observers that the line of the kings of Judah appears to continue through women expressly excluded by God's own laws. So what is going on? The inclusion of these prohibited gentile women is too frequent an event in the genealogical records to be a coincidence. God is clearly revealing it on purpose and following a divine plan. God is pointing to a greater law and deeper truth that he wants his people to grasp concerning the nature of the Bride.

Deut. 23:3 'No Ammonite may enter the Assembly of the LORD, even down to the tenth generation.'

The Ammonites came from the same background of perversion as the Moabites. Sexual impurity was actively present in their tribe from its birth. Even the offspring of the Ammonites were expressly forbidden from entering God's presence. It seems strange, therefore, that God purposefully includes these women in his family tree. Surely it must mean that he is unveiling the deep mystery of who is permitted to be

---

169   1 Kings 11:3

his Bride. God is indicating where she comes from and how she is to be accepted. From what can be read according to the Law of Moses concerning the Ammonites, Naamah should have been condemned and rejected. She was not worthy of consideration for marriage. Her people were vile and experts at mockery and ridicule and even mocked King David's servants by rejecting them, shaving them and leaving them naked.[170] The future prophets would denounce the Ammonites for their threats, taunts and insults.[171] They were a people famous for their cruel threats and malicious tongues.

Nevertheless, Naamah was chosen as a bride to belong to the King. Despite all the attributes of her former life being against her she was predestined to belong to the family of Jesus. There is always a greater law at work than the legalism of Judaism. God's greatest law is the law of love. The greatest command in God's word is always to love.[172] Naamah was loved and therefore would be accepted by the king. What is so wonderful is that this woman, whose tribe was renowned for having a foul mouth, would now belong to Solomon, a man whose tongue would utter some of the most beautiful speech ever recorded. The poetry Solomon gave to his bride is possibly the most intimate literature in Holy Scripture. A potentially foul-mouthed bride of Solomon would instead be remembered this way, 'Your lips are like a scarlet ribbon; your mouth is lovely.'[173] Like this Ammonite, the church of Christ has had her lips cleansed from the altar in the same way as Isaiah.[174] Fresh water now flows through her

---

170   1 Chron. 19:4
171   Zeph. 2:8
172   Matt. 22:37-39
173   Song of Songs 4:3
174   Isa. 6:7

mouth from her inner spring, instead of salty brine.[175] Many of God's people have often used their mouths to speak lies and profanity. Curses and slander flow with ease from an unclean Ammonite nature. After believing in Jesus some people still find it difficult to change their negative speech and may continue to bring harm through their mouths instead of goodness. The true Bride of Christ must remember that she is no longer an Ammonite. She now has the same graceful speech as her saviour and she blesses those around her, and she does not curse. Mockery and insult have no place in her life, as she is now joined to her Bridegroom whose word is always faithful and true. Just like her wise husband 'she speaks with wisdom, and faithful instruction is on her tongue.'[176]

Lot's wife

Gen. 13:7 'Quarrelling arose between Abram's herdsmen and the herdsmen of Lot. The Canaanites and Perizzites were also living in the land at that time.'

From what can be gleaned from scripture it would appear that Lot had no wife before he moved to Sodom. When Lot is next encountered he is married and living in the city of sin. Where he got his wife from cannot be precisely determined, but because it mentions that the Perizzites were in the land at the same time, it is probable that that Lot's wife was a Perizzite. The Perizzites were another one of the tribes from which the people of God were forbidden to take a wife. From what has been seen of God's mercy and grace in saving brides from condemned and rejected tribes, this should come as no surprise.

---

175   James 3:11
176   Prov. 31:26

The Bride in Sodom

2 Pet. 2:7-8 'He rescued Lot, a righteous man, who was distressed by the filthy lives of lawless men (for that righteous man, living among them day after day, was tormented in his righteous soul…)'

Despite much recent bad publicity concerning the character of Lot, it must be remembered that the Bible makes a clear statement that he was a 'righteous man.'[177] He may have made many mistakes during his lifetime, but he was living in a time of unprecedented wickedness amongst people of lawless immorality. In his distress he may have made unfortunate compromises, but amongst his confusion he still possessed a righteousness that came by faith in the one true God. It would appear that it is from amongst the very people of Sodom that Lot chose his bride. Marrying Lot was the wisest choice that his wife would ever make. Through marriage she would belong to this stranger of a different faith, who walked amongst the sinful Perizzites. He was very different from the other citizens of Sodom and his household would also be unique. By becoming his bride she would also come to understand something of Lot's real faith in the one true God.

Lot's bride had the same opportunities to be saved from her evil generation, as do the people of this present one. This present generation can also be saved from the coming destruction upon this world through belonging to someone who will betroth them to himself. Christ walks amongst the people of Sodom today. Scattered amongst the many sinful inhabitants of this world there are some who will see his difference, his otherworldly beauty. Hopefully they will enquire further about him, discover his love

---

177   2 Pet. 2:7

for them and then make the choice to belong to him. In doing so, they will choose to abide in his house, share in his life and be members of his church.

The Church in Sodom

Luke 17:32 'Remember Lot's Wife!'

At the house of Lot his family would break bread and wash feet.[178] In sharp contrast to the society around them, kindness and hospitality was a characteristic of the home of Lot and his wife. She would know something of the importance of hospitality and meaningful fellowship. She lived in the godliest building in the city and her home became a refuge from the evil practices of the town. She would also come to experience the fruitfulness of her bridegroom and bear children for him. Unfortunately, the church in Sodom had many problems. They were influenced by the prevailing spirit of the age, and the problems being encountered in the world were also infiltrating their home. Lot's daughters had made poor choices for their marriage partners and the church appeared to have no vision and was very materialistic. This small fellowship in Sodom may have believed the heresy that God's grace was a licence for immorality.[179] Sexual impurity, materialism and unclean associations were prevailing in Lot's house and the outpouring of God's wrath had finally arrived. It will be the same with the church at the end of this present age and the Bride must be ready to leave with her Bridegroom.

---

178   Gen. 19:2-3
179   Jude 1:10

Gen. 19:26 'Lot's wife looked back, and she became a pillar of salt.'

Despite all the opportunities afforded to Lot's bride, she was not going to make it. She would suffer a similar judgement to Sodom because that is where her heart really belonged. The bride in Sodom was attached to her possessions and the pleasures of that world more than to her bridegroom. God had chosen her out of the world and given her the gift of salvation, but her heart had turned back to the filth of the age. She was a lover of pleasure more than a lover of God. Jesus has warned his Bride many times that she must remain uncontaminated by this world. He has done everything possible to keep her clean and pure. He has purchased her, washed her and brought her into his house.

Sadly, there are many in his church that, despite having originally chosen to dwell in his house, have since turned back to the world in order to obtain the satisfaction that their heart craves. The true Bride of Christ is devoted to Jesus and does not love this world. No one can serve two masters[180] and no bride can belong to two men; she despises one and loves the other. It causes great pain to the heart of Jesus that many who claim to love him, turn away from their first love after making an initial commitment. The Bible is very clear that in the last days the love of many will grow cold.[181] Many will turn away from Jesus because they love their former life. Some churches will forsake their first love[182] and others will be attached to their wealth more than Christ.[183] A pig will go back to wallowing in the mire.[184] God does not wish his Bride to suffer wrath and

---

180   Matt. 6:24
181   Matt 24:12
182   Rev. 2:4
183   Rev. 3:17
184   2 Pet. 2:22

neither does he desire that any should perish, but the church must learn from the failure of Lot's wife. As in the days of Sodom, so it shall be in the days of the coming of Jesus.[185] Jesus comes to take his Bride out of this world and her heart must be pure and she must be ready. The true Bride's heart always belongs to her bridegroom and she will be ready to leave at the sound of his voice without looking back. She has no heart attachment to Sodom and no desire to live there. Given the choice she would prefer to settle in a city of peace, such as Jerusalem.

Jerusalem – The Once and Future Bride

Ezek. 16:3 'This is what the Sovereign LORD says to Jerusalem…Your father was an Amorite and your mother a Hittite.'

Judges 1:21 'The Benjamites failed to dislodge the Jebusites, who were living in Jerusalem; to this day the Jebusites live there.'

Rev. 21:2 'I saw the Holy City, the new Jerusalem, coming down out of heaven from God, prepared as a bride beautifully dressed for her husband.'

When the last two tribes on the list of prohibited brides are examined, something very interesting can be seen. The unclean Amorites and the stubborn Jebusites are both identified with the inhabitants of Jerusalem. The importance of Jerusalem in God's marriage plan cannot be overstated and his love for this unique city is constantly revealed in the Bible. The prophets continually spoke about this city's prophetic destiny in God's marriage plans. Isaiah prophesied of Jerusalem that 'as a bridegroom

---

185   Luke 17:30

116

rejoices over his bride so will your God rejoice over you.'[186] No other city in Scripture can be compared to Jerusalem. Jesus wept over it, taught it, cleansed it, died for it and is coming back to save it. It can plainly be seen in the Bible that Jerusalem is prophetically identified with the Bride of Christ. It is through God's love for Jerusalem that he reveals an insight into the past, present and future of his eternal Bride.

Jerusalem's Amorite Past

Ezek. 16:2-3 'Son of Man confront Jerusalem with her detestable practices and say...your father was an Amorite.'

Jerusalem originally came from the Amorites who in the past were a very sinful people. Even hundreds of years before Ezekiel confronted Jerusalem about her original ancestry,[187] God was taking note of her sins. Jerusalem was to be reminded that although its future could be blessed, its past was never acceptable to God. Ezekiel reminded Jerusalem that her favoured position was not due to any commendable actions on her own behalf. The prophet reminded Jerusalem by stating that she was unwashed, unclean, unclothed, despised, and cast out.[188] No one ever had compassion for her or took pity upon her. Whilst she was in this state of wretchedness the Lord passed by and saw her forsaken, naked and kicking about in her own blood and he declared that she 'live!' He then made her grow to become beautiful and fruitful. God lavished his love upon her, watched over her, clothed her, purchased her and entered into a solemn covenant of marriage with her. She was bathed in water and

---

186   Isa. 62:5
187   Gen. 15:16
188   Ezek. 16:4-5

adorned with jewellery. She was fed the finest food, became famous and as her beauty was made perfect, became the queen of all.[189]

God loved her more than all things and her despicable origins as an Amorite were forgotten. It is only after receiving all this grace and favour that the chilling indictment from the prophet of God is pronounced, 'but you trusted in your beauty and used your fame to become a prostitute.'[190] What follows is a catalogue of behaviour too disgusting for sensitive ears to hear. The sordid details of this fallen bride are recorded in Ezekiel's sixteenth chapter. In this long and sad lament God refers to her as an adulterous wife, a prostitute and a sister of Sodom.

It was at this very stage in Jerusalem's sinful life that another prophet, Jeremiah, was forbidden from taking a bride in that city.[191] Through his prophets God indicates his relationship to his people and clearly reveals that he will not take a Bride who continues in such sins. If addicted to sin, even Jerusalem 'who was queen among the provinces has now become a slave.'[192] It was possibly a mercy as well as a prophetic picture that Ezekiel's own beloved bride was taken away before the prophet was forced to watch God's wrath poured out on the fallen city of Jerusalem.[193] God always takes the true Bride away to his presence before the sinful are judged.

The church of today needs to be reminded of the prophet's warning to the Bride. Whilst believers may be highly favoured by God, their elevated status is the result of grace received from their Bridegroom who

---

189   Ezek. 16:6-14
190   Ezek. 16:15
191   Jer. 16:2
192   Lam. 1:1
193   Ezek. 24:16

loved them. God's abundant grace is never a licence for the Bride to be unfaithful. Believers must never assume that their unmerited favour means they can return to the uncleanliness of the Amorites. They have been set free from all of that. The church is the body of Christ and she is his holy temple.[194] His church must never allow itself to fall from its position as the favoured bride to become involved in spiritual adultery with this world or to prostitute itself with idols.

Jerusalem's Jebusite Present

Josh. 15:63 'Judah could not dislodge the Jebusites, who were living in Jerusalem; to this day the Jebusites live there with the people of Judah.'
Even after Joshua had conquered the Promised Land, the Jebusites still lived in Jerusalem. They stubbornly held on and never let go of the city despite onslaughts from the tribes of Israel. Although the Jebusites were surrounded by the Israelites they did not belong to God and didn't want him in their city. Jerusalem rested between two of the most prominent tribes who would produce the kings of Israel, Judah and Benjamin. They lived between the king who was and the one who would come. To the casual observer, Jerusalem could have been mistaken as belonging to Israel but in truth it refused to submit and held out as an enemy of God. The inhabitants of Jerusalem could have followed the example of Rahab and chosen to put their faith in the God of the people that surrounded them. Although coming from an unclean tribe, as did Rahab, they could have chosen to be saved by faith, but instead they opted to mock and ridicule the people of God. 'The Jebusites said to David, "You will not

---

194   1 Cor. 3:16-17

get in here; even the blind and the lame can ward you off."'[195] Like many unbelievers of today the Jebusites assumed that they alone controlled their own destiny and were content to laugh at the people of faith. They were totally unconcerned about the presence of David and ignored God's anointed king. They were not prepared to allow God's anointed into their city or invite him into their lives. They despised God's king and considered him weak and unimportant; someone who could easily be kept outside.

'Nevertheless, David captured the city.'[196] Despite what man thinks God has clearly said that Jerusalem belongs to him. The city is a picture of the Bride and Jesus, the greatest son of David, will always be victorious in claiming her for himself. It is unfortunate that many people today attend church but never allow the king inside their own lives. They may live in the midst of God's people but attending church does not mean belonging to it. The prophecy of scripture cannot be broken and Jerusalem will ultimately belong to Jesus, as his Bride. Everyone who inhabits a church building must ensure they also choose to belong to the one who owns the church. Jesus is coming to take his Bride just as surely as David came to take Jerusalem, and no one will ward him off. As the apostle John saw in the final revelation, Jerusalem will finally belong to Christ as a 'bride beautifully dressed for her husband.'[197]

---

195   2 Sam. 5:6
196   2 Sam. 5:7
197   Rev. 21:2

Jerusalem's Perfect Future

Rev. 21:9-10 'Come I will show you the bride, the wife of the Lamb.' And he carried me away in the Spirit...and showed me Jerusalem coming down out of Heaven from God.

Jesus will have his Bride. Although the consummation of this event is in the future, it is still an established fact in the eyes of God. In the book of Revelation John saw the final reality of the fulfilment of the purposes of God. Using established biblical metaphors the church's future is revealed. The Lamb is Jesus and Jerusalem is his Bride. Jesus is revealed as the author of time and space and the beginning and end co-exist with the eternal God.[198] The Bride comes from heaven to belong to the Lamb, Jesus. Just as the Lamb was slain before the foundation of the world,[199] so the Bride was chosen before the earth was created.[200] All true believers are 'born from heaven' and will consequently inhabit the New Jerusalem that 'comes down out of heaven.' The faithful Bride's heart is already in heaven from where her Bridegroom will come. Nothing can change these divinely ordained facts concerning the Bride's eternal future because God's word cannot be altered and the scriptures must be fulfilled. The Bride's destiny is settled and certain and she will belong to her Bridegroom. Through the Jerusalem to come, 'the dwelling of God is with men and he will live with them.'[201] The church of today must see the coming of Jesus as a certainty and she must confess it to be so. It is not only the Lord who eagerly awaits this approaching consummation, but the Bride also says "come!"[202]

---

198   Rev.1:8
199   Rev.13:8
200   1 Pet. 1:20
201   Rev. 21:3
202   Rev. 22:17

8

Brides of the Judges

While the young women were dancing, each man caught one and
carried her off to be his wife.
Judges 21:23

*I*n the times of Moses and the Judges God gave the brides great prominence. Although many Bible students focus mainly on the men of this historical period, God always makes sure that the essential nature of the woman is noted. When seeking to understand the mystery of the Bride, she can be clearly observed throughout the times of the Judges. During this dispensation examples are provided of women who overcome adversity and persevered in their faith to obtain the promises of God. Between the Exodus from Egypt and the time of Samuel, God's people were anticipating the arrival of the promised King of Israel.[203] God's chosen King and his bride would not arrive until the reign of David hundreds of years later. The brides before the time of the kingdom, however, are extremely important when seeking understanding of the full

---

203   Deut. 17:15

nature of the Bride of Christ. Many of the brides during this four hundred year dispensation were unnamed, but their deeds were still recorded by God. Many different aspects of the life of the Bride can be observed during this period. This includes Jephthah's virgin daughter,[204] (a picture of sacrifice, suffering and self-denial), to the brides of the Benjamites being 'caught up'[205] at the end of the dispensation. The church will similarly undergo trials, suffering and sacrifice until she is 'caught up'[206] to meet her bridegroom at the end of the church age. The ultimate reward of these women will be in joining the great multitude that have also been chosen to belong to God as part of his heavenly Bride. Some of these women have such noble characters that they demand closer attention. Starting from the time of Moses a sample of these brides will now be more closely examined.

Zipporah the Berated Bride

Exod. 2:21 'The man gave his daughter Zipporah to Moses in marriage. Zipporah gave birth to a son, and Moses named him Gershom, saying "I have become an alien in a foreign land."'

Whilst Israel suffered in bondage outside the Promised Land, their future leader Moses married Zipporah who was a Midianite. She was the bride of the man who would become the greatest Israelite of the age, but she was from a tribe considered to be outcasts. Midian's very name means 'strife and contention' and her tribe was birthed through Keturah, another

---

204   Judges 11:37
205   Judges 21:23
206   1 Thess. 4:17

wife of Abraham.[207] Despite their original links to the father of faith, the children of Isaac and Jacob viewed the Midianites with suspicion and mistrust. In the course of time they became despised enemies of the children of Israel and Gideon's army would fight against them driving them out of the Promised Land.[208] Zipporah may not have known it at the time, but her relationship to Moses would bring strife from within her own family circle. Her very existence would bring contention with some and even her children would not be free from certain aspects of this strife Num. 12:1 Miriam and Aaron began to talk against Moses because of his Cushite wife.

Some Bible scholars believe that Moses may have remarried by the time of the Exodus and that his Cushite wife referred to here is not Zipporah. Others think that this bride is the same woman and that she had Cushite as well as Midianite ancestry. Whatever her ethnicity, when Jesus chooses his Bride he also knows that she will never be accepted by some people. He has warned her very clearly that 'everyone will hate you because of me.'[209] There are many reasons why the church is despised, but when people hate his Bride Jesus takes it personally. Perhaps one reason for Miriam's displeasure was the primitive sin of racism. This specific evil afflicting the hearts of mankind never seems to be fully eradicated in even the most righteous of cultures. Despite racism stubbornly clinging to the fringes of many groups, it is undoubtedly hated and rejected by God. The simple glorious fact is, that with his blood Christ purchased his Bride

207   Gen. 25:2
208   Judges 7
209   Luke 21:17

'from every tribe and language and people and nation.'[210] The church is multi coloured, multinational, multilingual and ethnically diverse. The Bridegroom will never tolerate racial prejudice against his beloved.

Another reason for this strife and contention could be envy and jealousy. What is sad about this incident is that Miriam and the wife of Moses are both pictures of women accepted by God. Miriam was a good woman, a prophetess, who led praise and worship to the one true God.[211] She was saved and accepted by God, but through jealousy she was still incapable of accepting the fact that there was another lady close to the heart of God's great prophet. Similar conflict between godly women may be witnessed thousands of years later with Martha and Mary.[212] It is the same today with some churches failing to appreciate their own place in God's plan and failing to see their own unique ministries. Due to focusing on other people, they give way to jealousy and envy and criticise another part of the Bride of Christ. Instead of fostering notions of division, each individual fellowship should rejoice in the fact that all churches have unique and different relationships to the Bridegroom who loves them.

Another reason for this discord can come from an attitude of having superior moral and cultural standards. Perhaps Miriam felt justified in her criticism. After all, Moses' wife was not a true Israelite and it was well known that she only kept the covenant of circumcision reluctantly.[213] Miriam may have felt that this foreign woman didn't really want to keep the traditions of their forefathers. Miriam may also have felt that she

---

210   Rev. 5:9
211   Exod. 15:20
212   Luke 10:40
213   Exod. 4:25

was justified in her criticism on theological grounds. The prejudice of a church can be deep-rooted when it is backed up by their interpretation of an accepted denominational doctrine. Jesus was similarly criticised by such teachers of the law, and his true Bride can expect nothing less in this world. She is encouraged, however, to remember his words; 'if the world hates you, keep in mind that it hated me first.'[214] It is precisely because the Bride is accepted by God that she may be hated by the cold hearted theologians of this world who have no true relationship with the Bridegroom.

Whilst this disharmony is lamentable, perhaps the scriptures are unveiling something even more profound concerning the nature of God's Bride. Miriam was an Israelite and Moses' wife was not. Could it be that God was pointing towards a future relationship between his church and Israel? And that the envy in their relationship is a picture of the present division between the Jews and the Church? Perhaps God makes much of the church in the same way that Paul boasted of his ministry to the Gentiles, 'in the hope that I may somehow arouse my own people to envy and save some of them.'[215] God has offered salvation to both Israel and the gentiles. In a similar way both women in Moses' life would be saved, and both would ultimately belong to the same family of God. To Miriam Moses was her brother and the prophet and saviour of the nation, but to Zipporah Moses was 'a bridegroom of Blood.'[216] Moses loved both of them, but they are only a picture of all the people that God accepts through the saviour and Bridegroom Jesus Christ.

---

214   John 15:18
215   Rom. 11:14
216   Exod. 4:25

The story of Miriam's deliverance is well documented in scripture. She and her people had suffered terrible persecution at the hands of Egypt, but God poured out his plagues on the land and after much wrath and judgement, Israel was delivered from great tribulation into the promises of God. As it was then, so it will also be in the future; 'Israel will be saved.'[217] Despite God's great salvation from Egypt and wonderful promises for the future, Miriam's rebellious attitude would not be tolerated. Because of her actions, Miriam would have to suffer outside the camp for seven days until God's anger subsided, but she would still be accepted back into the camp because she was 'loved on account of the patriarchs.'[218] Here we find clear analogies pointing towards Israel's final deliverance out of a sevenfold period of tribulation when the wrath of God is poured out on the gentile world. This cannot be discussed in detail here, but one observation demands attention, and that is where Zipporah is during this time of Jacob's trouble in Egypt. The answer is that the bride is not there; she has been sent to a safe place.

Exod. 18:2 'Moses sent away his wife Zipporah and his father in law received her.'

Exod. 18:5 'Moses' father in law, together with Moses' sons and wife, came to him in the desert, where he was camped, near the mountain of God.'

Moses' sister would be delivered through the tribulation in Egypt, but the bride would be kept from it. Before God's wrath was poured out on

---

217   Rom. 11:26
218   Rom. 11:28

Egypt, Zipporah was sent away to safety at the father's house. Here can be seen a pattern of the Bride's protection from the time of the coming wrath. The Bridegroom sends his Bride to the father's house before God's judgement falls on this world.

'The Bridegroom sends his Bride to the Father's house before God's judgement falls on this world.'

The Bride's ultimate place of dwelling is always to reside at the Father's house. Jesus instructed His church that although he was going away to the Father's house he was preparing a place for his followers. He then informed them that he would come back and take them to be with him and the Father. Many types of persecution may befall the Bride in this world, but she will never suffer the wrath of God unleashed upon her. Her Bridegroom took the wrath of God upon himself in his body on the cross so that she would be protected from it.

What is equally illuminating in this story is who was present with Zipporah when she was sent into protection. There were three people with her: the father, the first born son, and Eliezer, which means 'God my helper.' The metaphors of the bride's companions are very encouraging. The church is not only in the protective care of the Father, but also of the Son and the Holy Spirit. The Bride always has access to, and fellowship with, each member of the Trinity.

It is also worthy of note, that after Israel was delivered from tribulation all those that belonged to God were brought out together to the great mountain of God's assembly. God keeps his promises to Israel and to his Bride. All who belong to him through the eternal covenant will be brought to the mountain of God. At this great and high mountain,[219] at the assembly of all the saints of God, the glory of the Bride will be seen just as described by John at the end of his revelation.[220] Despite her earthly trials the future of the Bride will be free of strife and conflict.

Acsah the Blessed Bride

Judges 1:12, 13 '"Caleb said, "I will give my daughter Acsah in marriage to the man who attacks and captures Kiriath Sepher." Othniel son of Kenaz, Caleb's younger brother, took it; so Caleb gave his daughter Acsah to him in marriage.'

Caleb is one of the great heroes in the Old Testament. His exploits are well documented and he is recorded as being someone who had a faith that pleased God. He followed God whole-heartedly and claimed Hebron – the resting place of Israel's fathers – as the inheritance for his family. Caleb was a great man of faith. And being a noble father, he would only allow his daughter to be given as a bride to a worthy husband. He declared that his daughter Acsah, his most treasured possession, would only be given to the man who could take Kiriath-Sepher, which means 'city of the book'.

Again is seen an unfolding picture of God's pattern for the Bride. Like Caleb, God the father has an inheritance to bestow, but the most precious gift of the Bride will only be given to the man who can win the battle and take the 'city of the book.' In Judges the man who triumphed was

---

219   Heb. 12:22-23
220   Rev. 21

Othniel of the tribe of Judah, whose name means the 'Lion of God.' The parallel is clear in revealing who the church will be given to. The Bride belongs to 'The Lion of the tribe of Judah, the root of David,' who 'hath prevailed to open the book'[221] It is Jesus, the only one who was worthy to open the book. He alone has won the victory and can claim the Bride from the Father. The Bridegroom and the Bride obtain an inheritance and they will live together in the place of their ancestors, which was given to them by the Father.

Judges 1:14-15 'When she came to Othniel she urged him to ask her father for a field...Caleb asked her, "what can I do for you?" She replied, "Do me a special favour...give me also springs of water." Then Caleb gave her the upper and lower springs."

After her bridegroom's victory Acsah appeared to have everything that she could desire: a great father, a perfect husband, and a place to live. Despite obtaining these precious possessions, she still asked for something more. She asked for water. Living in a dry and barren environment Acsah knew that she required a constant supply of water in order for life to continue. She started by asking her husband and then asked the father directly.

Over a thousand years later in Samaria, another woman would also request living water[222] from the 'lion of the tribe of Judah.' Jesus was always willing to supply living water to brides who asked and, two thousand years after the request of the Samaritan woman, believers in Christ should still be asking the Father to pour out the living water. Jesus

---

221   Rev. 5:5 (KJ)
222   John 4:15

told his church that they must ask for this water. He explained to the woman at the well that, 'whoever drinks the water that I give him will never thirst.'[223] He also shouted about this living water in Jerusalem so that the whole city could hear, 'If anyone is thirsty, let him come to me and drink…streams of living water will flow from within him.' He made it clear that this living water was the Holy Spirit.[224]

Jesus knows that his Bride must also have his Spirit flowing within her while she lives in the barrenness of this world. The church cannot survive or thrive without the living water of the Spirit flowing from within her. Acsah's life would have soon dried up and become like the desert waste around her without access to her father's springs of water. This principle is just as true for the church. To have a great Father and wonderful Bridegroom is not sufficient for the church to live the life to which it is called. She needs the spring, the stream, and the river of the Holy Spirit flowing within so that she will have a constant supply of refreshing life. Following Acsah's example, Jesus instructed his Bride to ask the Heavenly Father[225] for the supply of the Spirit. Both The heavenly Bridegroom and the Father promised that the Spirit would come to the church. The church relies on the Holy Spirit for its life and will soon die without his presence. The third member of the trinity is the gift from the Father and the Son[226] who supplies everything that the church needs for life and fruitfulness. He is not optional, His presence is essential and, like Acsah, the church must ask for Him.

---

223   John 4:14
224   John 7:37-38
225   Luke 11:13
226   John 15:26

Deborah the Battle Bride

Judges 4:4 'Deborah, a prophetess, the wife of Lappidoth, was leading Israel at that time.'

Judges 4:9-10 'Deborah said, "I will go with you"…Deborah went with Barak…men followed him and Deborah also went with him.'

For twenty years God's people were cruelly oppressed and they cried to the Lord for help.[227] His answer of deliverance came through a woman. Deborah would lead, direct and ride into battle with the army of God. Although the captain of the army would be Barak, which means 'lightning', Deborah would be at his side and, just as she prophesied, the enemy would be handed over to a woman. Exactly as she predicted, the battle of Deborah would be won on the plains next to Armageddon. The armies of God would conquer evil and the victory of this battle would become enshrined in the song of Deborah. It was not the first song of the Bride in scripture and it would not be the last. But it would one of the most prophetic being a declaration of the coming final battle of the Christ and his Bride at the end of time. God's Bride has been engaged in spiritual warfare for thousands of years and she is still undefeated.

Psalm 110:3 'Your troops will be willing on your day of battle. Arrayed in holy majesty, from the womb of the dawn.'

The song of Deborah in Judges chapter five gives very strong prophetic insights into the nature of the Bride of Christ. Deborah is no weak and feeble woman, incapable of proactive assertiveness. On the contrary, she is a mother, a strong prophetic leader, and a warrior; she is the picture of

---

227   Judges 4:3

Christ's church at the end of time. She fears no one but her God. When Deborah arose, war was declared, God's armies followed her, princes rode with her and 'from the heavens the stars fought'[228] on the side of the Bride. The thunder of the horses' hooves echoed across the valley of Armageddon and the angels spoke.[229] This was no ordinary conflict; it was the unveiling of the battle Bride. It is a picture of the future warrior princess who will ride with Christ when her Bridegroom appears, like 'lightning'[230] at the end of this age on the great and dreadful day of the LORD.

Rev. 19:7-8 'His bride has made herself ready. Fine linen, bright and clean was given her to wear.'

Rev. 19:13-14 'His name is the Word of God. The armies of heaven were following him, riding on white horses and dressed in fine linen, white and clean.'

John saw the final battle at the end of time and recorded the details in the book of Revelation. Most people know that Christ rides to victory at his second coming. Many understand that the King of Kings returns to defeat all evil and establish righteousness upon the earth. Some, however, appear to have missed the fact that someone is riding into battle at his side. These riders are not named, but a precise description of their clothing is provided. They are portrayed as wearing wedding garments, the clothes of the Bride. When Jesus returns in victory he is coming to share his conquest with his Bride. Prophetically, Deborah sang about the

---

228   Judges 5:20
229   Judges 5:22-23
230   Luke 17:24

Bride being followed by the armies of heaven. Solomon also sang this prophetic song when the bridegroom declared that his bride is 'Lovely as Jerusalem, majestic as troops with banners.'[231] The Bride of Christ, like Deborah the prophetess, has already seen the future and knows that the victory with her Bridegroom is an established fact. The Church should always be ready for the coming battle because she knows that she is already more than a conqueror through him that loved her.[232]

Jael the Brave Bride

Judges 5:24 'Most blessed of women be Jael, the wife of Heber the Kenite, most blessed of tent dwelling women.'

It is easy to see in the book of Judges that victory for God is often obtained at the hands of a woman. Deborah has already been looked at, but there are other examples. The mighty Samson was defeated by Delilah,[233] and the false leader Abimelech was killed as a result of a head wound at the hands of a woman.[234] Like Shebna, who opposed David, false leaders are often defeated by head wounds at the hands of women.[235] Perhaps even the 'Antichrist beast', who is yet to come, will receive his fatal blow from a Bride who will recognise his evil intentions.[236] The true Bride of Christ only recognises one head[237] and ruler over her life and she knows how to deal with all false claims of headship. Jael is a wonderful example of a bride from the time of the judges who was not afraid to deal with evil

---

231   Song of Songs 6:4
232   Rom. 8:37
233   Judges 16:19-20
234   Judges 9:53
235   2 Sam. 20:22
236   Rev. 3:3
237   Eph. 5:23

when it raised its head.

Jael was married to Heber whose name means 'fellowship.' Here is a bride who is married to a man whose very name is hospitable, and her habit of opening up her home to strangers is commendable. Jael is also praised for being the most blessed of those living in tents. Likewise, the church must always be open to strangers in need and ready to provide help to those who require food and shelter, just as Jael was. Some churches in the book of Acts were planted when God-fearing women invited apostles of Christ into their homes.[238] The story of this bride, however, reveals something equally important about what God desires to see in his church. Jael soon discerned that this visitor in her tent was taking advantage of her hospitality whilst harbouring evil in his heart. He did not have pure motives for being with her, and this woman of God was ready to take the action that was required to remove this wickedness from her household.

Judges 4:21 'Jael, Heber's wife, picked up a tent peg and a hammer and went quietly to him while he lay fast asleep, exhausted. She drove the peg through his temple into the ground, and he died.'

Jael was friendly and hospitable but she was nobody's fool. She was kind and open to helping those in need, but she soon spotted a man who had come to take advantage of a woman's kindness. It is a sad fact that many 'false brethren'[239] often infiltrate the church. These wolves in sheep's clothing may appear weak and harmless at first, as did Sisera, but inwardly they are ravenous wolves come to devour the flock.[240] God will punish any man who comes into his tent to take advantage of his

---

238   Acts 16:15
239   2 Pet. 2:1
240   Acts 20:29

Bride's kindness. His discerning Bride has also learned to spot when troublemakers with impure motives are present in the church.

Jael was a true and noble bride; kind and hospitable, but ready to deal with traitors in the camp. Sisera may have thought that he was safe with his secret identity hidden in the tent of this bride, but he was deluded. Jael was not going to allow her house to become polluted by this vile man. This courageous woman loved her God and she loved her household too much to allow it to be ruined by the presence of evil imposters. She took swift action and the problem was eradicated. The true Bride of Christ loves her Bridegroom too much to allow another man to take advantage of her house. She is filled with authority and strength and is empowered by her Lord. All power has been given to her to use this authority in keeping her house clean. She does this through hospitality, kindness and grace, but she 'cannot tolerate wicked men...those who claim to be apostles but are not, and [are] false.'[241] She knows that her Bridegroom has authorised his Bride to 'expel the wicked man from among you.'[242] She faithfully obeys and her house is kept clean for her husband to return.

Naomi the Bitter Bride

Ruth 1:20 "Don't call me Naomi," she told them. "Call me Mara (bitter), because the Almighty has made my life very bitter."'

Nothing is recorded in scripture that suggests any serious faults in the character of Naomi. Her conduct described in the book of Ruth, reveals a woman who has genuine faith and hope in the God of Israel. Nevertheless,

---

241   Rev. 2:2
242   1 Cor. 5:13

her life turned out to be full of pain, mourning and loss. Naomi lived 'in the days when the Judges ruled,'[243] and her story begins with a famine and a journey out of the Promised Land to live as an alien amongst the cursed Moabites. She may not have even planned any of these events herself, but may simply have followed the direction and authority of her husband Elimelech. Unfortunately, any project or plan that is outside the guidance and promise of God is always doomed to failure. God expects his people to use faith during times of famine not unbelief, and he does not expect people to escape from responsibility into another land. Naomi was carried along by a vision that was false and into a life for which she was never called. Unbelief and departure from God ultimately leads to death, and, consequently, her husband and two sons died. Her life became consumed with mourning and loss without any visible prospect of improvement. What made it more bitter may have been that all Naomi had done was follow the guidance of her husband and leader Elimelech. Many Christians today carry within them a similar bitter experience to Naomi. They understand their position in Christ, but also know that they should obey authority and submit to the leaders in their life of faith. They faithfully follow the Elimelechs in their life even when having doubts concerning the direction they are taking the church. Elimelech's false enterprise would result in the death of his children and leave Naomi a widow and an alien. Sadly, some pastors similarly lead the church into doomed projects with the result being that some people are lost and others become bitter.

The outcome of such faulty and uninspired leadership is that many

---

243   Ruth 1:1

Christians feel just like Naomi, alone, empty and bitter. Any Christian who has experienced similar disappointment in their walk of faith should learn the lesson of Naomi. Although she was a widow, there was someone watching over her who always noticed the widows.[244] Jesus never sees anyone purely as a widow, but he sees someone who has the potential to become part of his Bride.

Ruth 1:6 'She heard in Moab that the LORD had come to the aid of His people.'

Despite all the bitterness within her, she heard the good news that 'The Lord had come.' Whatever pain a church has gone through it must remember who the real leader of the Bride is. No leader or pastor, good or bad, has ownership of the church. The Bride of Christ has no earthly husband with faulty visions and actions, because she belongs to Jesus. Any disappointed and downcast believer must hear the word of God afresh, as Naomi did. The Bridegroom always comes for the Bride and he comes, first of all, through his word.

Jesus is the word of God. When the Bride puts aside the failings of her former leaders and listens to the words of the coming Bridegroom, she has already started her journey of faith back to the provision of God. It must have been hard to begin another journey after all she had been through, but Naomi had to get back to the place where God could bless her. She had to leave Moab and settle in Bethlehem, the place where the promise of God would be birthed. Even as she began this difficult journey there were still many unanswered questions in her life. She did not know where she

---

244   Luke 21:2

would reside, how she would make a living, or who would sustain her in old age, but she did not let these problems hamper her resolve to return to God. The journey of faith always has such questions invading the mind, but only one thing was necessary, Naomi had to trust and obey God and get back to the place of blessing. Once a church has obeyed as Naomi did, the heavenly Bridegroom begins to unleash his divine provisions that ensure his Bride will be fruitful. Naomi would ultimately inherit a new life that was more blessed than her former existence.

Ruth 4:16 'The woman living there said, "Naomi has a son."'
Naomi's obedience and faith continued to move forward until God's promise arrived and a son was born. Strictly speaking, Naomi did not have a son, it was Ruth's son, but that is not what was recorded or what people said. Gentile Ruth and Jewish Naomi worked together and so the son belonged to both women. When believers work together, everyone rejoices because God blesses his true Bride regardless of the denominational name she has been given by men.

Naomi would belong to a larger family and the older generation would be united with the younger one. There would be a new leader for the bride, Boaz of Bethlehem, who was a strong man of God. The famine was over, the bride was redeemed and a new inheritance was given. Naomi now had a hope and a future and just as God's word confirmed, she would forget the reproach of her widowhood because the Lord was now her husband.[245] More importantly than all the individual blessings of these women was the fact that new life would be born through God's Bride. A

---

245   Isaiah 54:4-5

son was now born and David would soon arrive. This coming king would also be a picture of the great royal bridegroom who is coming to take his Bride.

Hannah the Barren Bride

1 Sam. 1:5 'To Hannah he gave a double portion because he loved her, and the LORD had closed her womb.'

The theme of the barren bride is a repeated pattern throughout the Bible. In all the different dispensations God places special emphasis on childless women, including: Sarah, Rebekah, and Rachel during the time of the Patriarchs; Hannah and Manoah's wife in the reign of the Judges; the Shunammite in the period of the prophets; and Elizabeth at the incarnation. Barrenness was considered a curse by the Israelites because God himself had said that through his blessing no one would be barren.[246] Despite the curse of barrenness, God's chosen brides are continually discovered to be childless, almost as a prerequisite for the fulfilment of his divine plan. The reality of barrenness is an essential aspect to be grasped concerning the unfolding mystery of the Bride of Christ.

Hannah knew she was loved[247] but she also understood that she was created for something more. Her husband Elkannah was a righteous man who loved and cared for his wife. His name means 'God has purchased' and he is a wonderful picture of Jesus, who purchased his Bride with his own blood. Hannah knew her husband was good, but she still craved something more. She longed to bear children and be fruitful for her

---

246   Exod. 23:26
247   1 Sam. 1:5

husband. This pain of barrenness would increase as the years went by. She would eventually reach breaking point in her desperation to birth a child and would cry out to God through fasting, weeping and prayer. Her grief and passion in seeking God would become so intense that even good people would misinterpret her motives.[248] It did not matter to Hannah, she knew that the woman was created to be fruitful and every member of God's church also appreciates this inner longing.

1 Sam. 1:6 'Because the LORD had closed her womb, her rival kept provoking her in order to irritate her. This went on year after year.'
Hannah was deeply irritated due to being continually mocked by people who considered themselves more blessed than she. The years of this provocation built up within her soul until she was like a volcano ready to explode. It was not just her own ability that was being mocked, but the very promises of God were being ridiculed and she could stand it no longer. 'The barren womb is never satisfied.'[249] She refused to eat, began to pray and poured out her soul with such anguish and desperation that the high priest heard her request.

When the church wakes up to the reality of its own barren situation, it will also cry out to God. Sadly, many in the church are unaware and unconcerned about their barrenness. Too many Christians are content to be loved by God and satisfied with his gracious provision. For many Christians being fruitful for Jesus is not a priority in their lives.

The true Bride of Christ, however, follows the example of Hannah and

---

248   1 Sam. 1:14
249   Prov. 30:16

the other barren women of God in the Bible. She knows that being barren is a mockery of God and his promises. Jesus had promised that his church would be fruitful and anything less than this is an insult to his word. The Bride is not being selfish in attitude here; she is determined to bring honour to her Bridegroom and obtain the fruit that she was ordained to bear. Through prayer, tears, fasting and intercession the real Bride of Christ cries out until the high priest in heaven hears her voice. Christ, God's high priest, always sees the tears and hears the prayers of his Bride. Despite the 'pains in childbearing'[250] the Bride will give birth to life and glorify God.

1 Sam. 1:19 'Elkanah lay with Hannah his wife, and the LORD remembered her. So in the course of time Hannah conceived and gave birth to a son.'

Three people were essential to the conception of Hannah's child: the high priest heard her prayer, God remembered, and her husband loved her. The result was that Hannah was fruitful and birthed a son. Through her determination and prevailing prayer this woman of God obtained the promise and blessing that she desired. After the success of this prayer she prophesied that 'she who was barren has borne seven children.'[251] Increased prayer brings increased faith. When the church follows Hannah's example, she too will find that God will make sure that her tears and intercession will bring forth fruit.

Through her faith Hannah birthed Samuel the greatest prophet and judge

---

250   Gen. 3:16
251   1 Sam. 2:5

that Israel would know in that generation. He would guide and save the nation from their enemies and would anoint David, the man after God's own heart, to be king. None of these events, that were essential to God's plan, could have occurred unless Hannah had prayed. As Jesus reminded his disciples,[252] nothing can defeat a praying woman. When the church prays a nation can be changed, God's word can be heard, and the King can come. When the promised King finally arrives he will require a royal bride.

---

252   Luke 18:1-8

9

The Royal Bride

'At your right hand is the royal bride in Gold of Ophir. Listen, O daughter, consider and give ear: Forget your people and your father's house. The king is enthralled by your beauty; honour him, for he is your lord.'

Psalm 45:9-10

*A*fter the brides during the times of the Judges, the story of God's search for the perfect Bride soon brings the revelation that she is destined for royalty. In addition to her regal call, God's longing for the Bride is often expressed with reference to her always being acknowledged as beautiful. His words are written to enable her to understand his deep longing for her in the hope that she will leave her earthly house to be united with him in the King's palace. In looking at the wives of King David as a type of the church God desires, a picture can be seen of the Bride that God is seeking. The church of Jesus Christ is destined to be a beautiful royal bride.

Bathsheba

She Stood

1 Kings 1:28 'King David said, "Call in Bathsheba." So she came into the king's presence and stood before him."

It has already been shown how beautiful Bathsheba was taken from the Hittites and given to the tribe of Judah. After this unfortunate and confusing affair was put behind her, Bathsheba was later revealed as the queen, the most favoured bride of the King David. The continuation of Bathsheba's story serves as a parable for everyone who belongs to Jesus Christ. Just like Bathsheba, all Christians have left their former unclean condition and have now been united with the King.

The story of Bathsheba, however, does not end with her being taken as a bride of King David. Although she achieved ultimate status as the royal bride, she still had an essential function to fulfil. In a similar way to Esther, another beautiful royal bride who saved her people, Bathsheba utilised her privileged position to enter the king's presence and ensure God's will was carried out. Like these royal brides, believers enjoy the greatest privilege in all of God's creation. The Bride of Christ is unique in its intimacy with God and of being able to stand in his presence and approach his throne to obtain favour.[253] Scripture is clear that when Christ's Bride stands before her Bridegroom and king, he extends to her the sceptre of grace and favour. The church must likewise make essential use of this honoured position in order to ensure that God's kingdom is extended.

---

253   Heb. 4:16

She Knelt

1 Kings 1:16 'Bathsheba bowed low and knelt before the king. "What is it you want?" the king asked.

In approaching David, as his wife, Bathsheba still acknowledged that her beloved was also God's chosen and anointed King. The church must never abandon its humility and reverence when approaching its bridegroom. Bowing low was often considered an act of worship in the Old Testament[254] and it is right and fitting that Bathsheba pay correct honour to the king when in his presence. When believers understand that they are called to belong to the Bride of Christ, they should never assume that this relationship should deteriorate into informal familiarity when in the king's presence. In many natural marriage partnerships, husbands and wives can often fail to respect and appreciate the other's presence. This must never become the case between Jesus and his Bride. The head of the church, whilst being the Bridegroom, is also the holy and anointed Son of God. Whilst accepting her position as his Bride, correct protocol for the church is always to bow in reverence and worship when in the presence of Jesus.

When in David's presence, Bathsheba had also learned to be confident in asking for God's will to be done in her life. This assertive position may have initially been hard for Bathsheba to undertake. In her previous life she appeared to have led a very passive existence. Her beauty often meant that she was used as a pawn in the hands of powerful men. She may have become accustomed to this cycle of being used and it could have been safer to just let people have their way with her in the hope that everything

---

254   Gen. 24:26

would turn out all right in the end. Her life's experiences, however, had taught her much and something had changed in Bathsheba's character. She was no longer a naïve young girl, but she now recognised that she was the royal bride, a woman with authority, and she was going to wield her power. She had already obtained promises from the king concerning her children and she was going to make sure David kept his word and that God's will was done. The church follows her example in approaching Jesus and claiming all his promises.

1 Kings 1:17 'She said to him, "My Lord, you yourself swore to me your servant by the Lord your God.'"

Despite a period of settled calm and prosperity, everything again seemed to be going wrong in Bathsheba's world. King David's original word to her was not being obeyed, and another usurper to the throne had claimed the position previously promised to her son Solomon. Whilst in the presence of the King, Bathsheba reminded him of his own word to her. She knew who she was and she was bold enough to remind David of his original promise to her that their son Solomon would be the next king. She would not leave his presence until the King ratified this word and she would make sure that other witnesses heard it. She would ensure that the King fulfilled his word by using his power and authority. Let no one underestimate the power of a persistent woman. Jesus said that through her persistence she will prevail, even against an unrighteous ruler; how much more so with a righteous king.[255]

The Bride of Christ has to learn that she has power when in the presence

---

255   Luke 18:1-8

of her Bridegroom. She must use her assertive position to prevail with the king. She should also lay hold of the promises given by her lord and kneel before him and prevail upon him to fulfil his word through power and action. Jesus, just like David, is more than willing to listen and carry out his Bride's requests when she reminds him of his promises. Let every believer follow Bathsheba's example and assertively acknowledge their powerful position as part of the Bride. Let everyone kneel in Christ's presence and insist that he fulfil his word in extending his kingdom, protecting his Bride, and promoting his children. When hearing his own word of truth on the lips of his beloved, the king loves to grant the requests of his royal Bride.

She Sat

1 Kings 2:19 'Bathsheba went to King Solomon to speak to him…the king stood up to meet her, bowed down to her and sat down on his throne. He had a throne brought for the king's mother, and she sat down at his right hand.'

The last picture of Bathsheba in the Old Testament confirms her regal elegance. No woman enjoyed a higher status than she. Her actions and dignity had led her to be seated upon a royal throne at the right hand of the king. She was given the reward she had earned and was praised by the elders of the land.[256]

Just like the church, Bathsheba did not always make wise decisions in life and did not always make correct requests. She once asked the king to do something against his will and Solomon was forced to overrule

---

256   Prov. 31:31

her petition.[257] The church often makes similar mistakes when she acts without consulting the king. Nevertheless, her position as a royal queen was settled and established, just as the church is secure in her position as the Bride of Christ. Solomon's throne would be totally secure throughout his reign and the extension of his kingdom continued to increase. The next generation would enjoy a reign of peace thanks to the actions of this royal bride. Like Bathsheba, the royal Bride at the king's side, the church is also invited to be enthroned with Christ in heavenly realms.[258]

Abigail

1 Sam. 25:3 'His name was Nabal and his wife's name was Abigail. She was an intelligent and beautiful woman, but her husband…was surly and mean in his dealings.'

Abigail's destiny was to become a beautiful royal bride of King David. She did, however, have one big problem in her life that would stop her destiny from being fulfilled. She was already married to Nabal, a foolish man.

Her present marital status was not the only problem prohibiting Abigail from belonging to David, but Nabal's character was also a daily trial. She was married to a fool and she had no option but to acknowledge it.[259] There was nothing pleasant about Abigail's husband. Despite being blessed with riches, he was mean, ungracious, ungodly, arrogant, and proud. Nabal acted as if he were a king. He ignored David, God's true king, and was prepared to insult him by boasting that he wasn't important.

---

257   2 Kings 2:22
258   Eph. 2:6
259   1 Sam. 25:25 Nabal means 'fool'

In contrast to the wicked nature of Nabal, his bride was beautiful and intelligent with a great destiny planned for her life.

Abigail gives a perfect illustration of the predicament faced by every believer in Christ. All Christians are beautiful in God's sight with a great destiny planned for their life. Unfortunately they are constantly reminded of their attachment to the wicked fool of their old carnal nature that spoils the good things that Jesus has to offer. So many of God's people have obtained great promises from the Lord and know that he loves them, but they are continually hampered by their old sinful nature that insists on ruining God's future for them. Just when David appears on the horizon and promises a greater life, up pops the wicked old fool Nabal who stops Abigail form moving into her destiny.

Just as Abigail had no power to stop Nabal, a Christian cannot reform or change their old self, because the sinful nature listens to no one. Divorce was not permitted for Abigail and even if this occurred, David may not want to risk marring a woman who still legally belonged to such a man. The situation seemed hopeless for Abigail, as her life was bound to Nabal along with the drudgery of obeying his controlling and dominating influence in her life. She felt trapped by this attachment to Nabal and many believers feel the same today. They seem incapable of breaking their habits, addictions and thought patterns. Their desires of the sinful nature scream and demand attention and they feel compelled to obey. There was, however, a way of escaping from this cycle of slavery for Abigail.

1 Sam. 25:39 'David heard that Nabal was dead...then David sent word to Abigail, asking her to become his wife.'

Marriage is only until death. 'A married woman is bound to her husband as long as he is alive, but if her husband dies, she is released.'[260] The binding law of marriage ends at death. Abigail would be delivered from slavery to her old sinful husband, but it would not be through reforming or improving him, it would be through his removal and death.

> *'The sinful old man cannot trouble the new Bride any more, as he is dead.'*

This would not be through murder or any wrongdoing on Abigail's part. God would judge Nabal and his own sin would result in his demise. His heart of stone would fail, and Abigail would be free to marry again. With the removal of Nabal there was only one man she desired. It was the coming king, the one who had spared her life, and the one she had chosen to serve. David would come to take her to be his bride and Nabal would be mentioned no more.

When Jesus liberates his Bride he does not save the sinful nature of her carnal self, he saves his people 'from their sins.'[261] Nabal may have become 'one flesh' with Abigail but for a believer in Christ, their 'old man is crucified with him, that the body of sin might be destroyed.'[262] Abigail would be freed through the death of her 'old man', just as a believer is set free by their sinful nature being crucified with Christ. The sinful old man cannot trouble the new Bride any more as he is dead. God judged him and

---

260   Rom. 7:2
261   Matt. 1:21
262   Rom. 6:6

removed him. The new Bridegroom, however, is alive! As it was true for Abigail, so it is true for the church.

After becoming aware of these momentous events in her life Abigail still had a duty to perform. She needed to act quickly upon her new situation and circumstances and seize the opportunity David was now presenting her with

1 Sam. 25:42 'Abigail quickly got off her donkey and, attended by her five maids, went with the king's messengers and became his wife.'

God had worked all things together for good for[263] Abigail because he loved her. She would be a perfect royal bride for God's chosen king. Despite all things being fulfilled, Abigail still had to move into her new destiny. First of all she had to believe that everything that David had said was true. By faith she had to accept that she was indeed called to belong to God's future king. It may have taken time for her to accept the fact that her 'old man' was really dead and that now she was called to become 'one flesh' with a new man, the coming king. It may have all sounded too good to be true, but it was all very real. God's call for all believers to now become his Bride is also true. The 'Old Man'[264] of sin is really dead, Jesus put him to death on the cross and by law the old marriage was ended. The Bride who was once enslaved to that old nature is now free to belong to Christ.

Abigail, with her five maids, had to leave her old home of mourning and death and depart to be with David. The time was soon approaching

---

263   Rom 8:28
264   Eph. 4:22 K.J.

when she would live in a palace with the king as the royal bride, but this would only be fulfilled if she left the present house of Nabal. The Bride of Christ is always called to leave her old life and be transformed by the resurrected life of her new bridegroom. This takes determined actions on the part of the church. Believers have to move out of real circumstances linked to their old life before they can move into God's new provision. Jesus made it very clear that those who belong to him must follow him to be where he is. This sometimes included leaving homes, family and occupations in order to be united with him.

It is interesting that Abigail took five maids with her when leaving to become David's bride. When Jesus talked about his coming wedding banquet he stressed that, although many were invited, only five of the bridesmaids were ready to leave.[265] This is very sobering when considering Christ's words that, 'many are called, but few are chosen'. The Bride is called to leave this world and go to the Father's house. This calling must never be forgotten or relegated to being a minor doctrine of the church. It requires determined activity on the part of believers to ensure they are ready to leave everything of the old nature when the Bridegroom calls.

David had rescued Abigail from her previous life and he would always be there to save her from trouble. Years later when she was captured by the Amalekites, David would again quickly come to her rescue and save his bride from this carnal tribe.[266] Abigail never needed to be afraid of future trouble. Her husband was the coming king and the greatest warrior in Israel. Those who attempt to kidnap the royal bride are ultimately

---

265   Mat. 25:1-13
266   1 Sam. 30:5

destroyed. David was a true husband who protected his bride just as his greater ancestor Jesus Christ always rescues and protects his church.

Michal

1 Sam. 18:28 'The LORD was with David...and Michal loved David.'

Michal did not marry into royalty she was born into it. As daughter of King Saul she was brought up as a princess and she probably dreamed of the day when her noble prince would arrive. One day he did appear and Michal married David who was destined to become the future king. She was genuinely in love with him. He was the hero of Israel, a warrior poet and was now her husband. David would love her, he would fight for her and he would sing for her. Life could not have worked out better for Michal and surely everything that she had hoped for had come to pass. Her new life with David had begun perfectly, but days of testing were still to come. It would be how she would handle the trials ahead that would prove whether she would become a fruitful bride of the King. It is the same with the church; good beginnings do not automatically result in happy endings. Many Christians begin their life with Christ with good intentions, but like the good seed in Jesus' parable, the 'worries of this life and deceitfulness of wealth choke it, making it unfruitful.'[267] Many believers start off well, but quickly fall away when trouble comes. Michal's time of testing was about to begin.

---

267   Mat. 13:22

Test of Loyalty

1 Sam. 19:11 'Saul sent men to David's house...to kill him...but Michal, David's wife warned him...run for your life.'

It soon became clear that Michal's father did not like David. Saul was not just Michal's dad, but he was also the existing king. Her loyalties would be tested as to who she would belong to and which kingdom she would choose to live in. At first glance her actions in trying to protect her husband may appear noble, but it must be remembered that when David fled for his life to live in the desert, Michal chose to stay at the palace instead of joining her husband in his life and ministry. Unfortunately, Michal tried to appease both men by attempting to be loyal to her father whilst helping her husband at the same time. This division in her loyalty ended up spoiling her relationship with her bridegroom David, the future King. Many Christians do love God, but when the real choices have to be made between sacrificial service and home comforts many stay at home often out of a misguided sense of loyalty. Perhaps Michal preferred being royal to being loyal. She may have lost her bridegroom, but she still had a royal title and was still a princess. However, she would soon discover that disconnecting from God's chosen bridegroom would mean losing everything.

Christians are called to be loyal to their heavenly Bridegroom and maintain their relationship to him at all costs. Jesus will ensure that their royal status is protected and confirmed, but he is seeking a loyal Bride. If the Bride won't be loyal she is not fit to be royal. Sadly, many believers prefer to hold on to their status in life rather than follow Jesus through the desert of sacrifice and ministry. When someone chooses to belong to Christ they pledge their loyalty to him. They cannot follow two masters and they must not attempt to please two different kings. The Bride is called to leave her former household and to cleave to her husband.[268] If a believer attempts to appease both their former king as well as their new king, all that will be achieved is an erosion of their relationship to their new bridegroom. The consequences of this can be catastrophic for the Bride.

Test of Relationship

1 Sam. 25:44 'Saul had given his daughter Michal, David's wife, to Paltiel son of Laish.'

Because of her divided loyalties Michal now found that her situation became much worse. All of her existing relationships would now deteriorate as she became disconnected from her bridegroom. Michal's confidence in her father, God's rejected king, was badly misplaced. Saul was a shrewd political leader and his charisma deceived many. Even Michal's brother, the noble Jonathan, chose to stay with Saul instead of following David, God's true anointed king. Remaining faithful to failed denominational structures instead of following the leading of God's anointing is a misguided and doomed policy of obedience.

Many good people are led astray by deceitful leaders. Michal's father now directed her life by manipulating her in a way that she would never have chosen. If she had opted to stay with David, she would never have suffered this shame. The king of this world is also a dictator and, whilst

---

268   Gen. 2:24

pretending to help, will always control and abuse people away from their God ordained destiny. The true Bridegroom never behaves like this. The terrible consequences of Michal's divided heart would result in her being given to another bridegroom. Her life entered a spiral of confusion that would make no sense and had no future. To make things even worse, another man now controlled her life; a husband she never wanted.

Little is known about her life during those long wasted years. Perhaps she tried to make the best of her new marriage, but it was likely tainted with the regret of losing David. Each passing day may have made her original vow of loyalty to David seem more like a distant dream. Perhaps she heard the rumours that David had married another wife in the desert.[269] This would compound her misery and confirm her belief that the life she had dreamed of as David's future royal bride, was completely over.

Many Christians have fallen into similar dejection and depression when life takes a wrong turn. Realising that they have made bad choices in life and failed to follow God whole-heartedly, many believers have given up hope of expecting any improvement in their situation. Worse still, many know that it is entirely their fault for failing to keep their vows to Christ and allowing themselves to be separated from their Bridegroom. Despite all these years of regret and gloom there was, nevertheless, something that Michal may not have dared to believe. It is something that many Christians also often fail to remember. The King was coming back, and the first thing he would ask for was his bride.

---

269   1 Sam. 25:43

The Test of Repentance

2 Sam. 3:14 David sent messengers to Ish-bosheth son of Saul, demanding, "Give me my wife Michal, whom I betrothed to myself.'

Jesus is coming back and he is going to claim his Bride, woe to anyone who gets in his way. David was coming to take his throne and kingdom back. His first demand would be that his bride was presented to him. Many years had passed and some people had forgotten or failed to believe that he was coming back, but God's promise was that David would be king, and his word is always true. There was going to be trouble if Michal was not returned to David.

The news of David's return must have come as a tremendous shock to Michal. She was probably bewildered that David still wanted her after all these years. She had been disloyal to David and had now given her life to someone else. Maybe she had even forgotten about her former marriage covenant to David, as the long years of separation could have eaten into her memory. Perhaps she did not love David anymore or even think about him. Whatever she may have felt, one thing was certain, David had not forgotten. He had never given up on his marriage vows and Michal was betrothed to him, as he had purchased her for himself.[270] David served an ultimatum to the leaders of the kingdom that they must return his bride. No one was strong enough to disobey David and no one dare challenge his authority. Michal's replacement husband, Paltiel, might be hurt by it[271] but it was the consequence of taking the king's bride for himself. He ought to have been thankful that David did not take his life.

---

270   1 Sam. 18:25-27
271   2 Sam. 3:16

Whatever condition believers find themselves in during this life, let them be certain of one unchangeable fact: Jesus is coming back for his Bride and an extended period of time between his betrothal and arrival will not change the certainty of this outcome. A church may have let its love grow cold, but he never forgets his marriage agreement and his love for his Bride never grows dim. His betrothal covenant was ratified and confirmed when he purchased his church with his own blood. Christ is coming for his Bride; this is certain, and no one has the authority to stop it.

The Test of Attitude

2 Sam. 6:16 'As the Ark of the LORD was entering the city of David, Michal daughter of Saul watched from a window. And when she saw King David leaping and dancing before the LORD, she despised him in her heart.'

Michal still had the opportunity to return to her perfect life when her marriage to the king was restored. All God's promises could have still been outworked for her, but unfortunately her love for David had changed over the years. Her love for other things may have affected her attitude, or maybe she had just abandoned her faith in what God originally had planned for her. Either way, Michal had allowed bitterness to enter her heart and this cancer of the soul will always produce barrenness. She may have felt justified in passing judgement on others, as she had been through a lot of trouble in life. Hard-hearted and bitter people are always good at justifying themselves. One thing had become very clear, her love had grown cold, or it had been abandoned, and she was now content to rest in her own sense of self-righteousness.

Interestingly, the Bible calls Michal 'the daughter of Saul' instead of the wife of David and this was the true disposition of her heart. It appeared that Michal could not let go of her past, which resulted in her despising the new things that God was doing in her life. When everyone was rejoicing in the presence of God, which is what the Ark represents, she was looking down on it and watching the proceedings with a judgemental eye. Michal was not going to join in with this new style of worship because she felt it was beneath her royal standing, but deity seldom meets with dignity. She valued religious procedures of men, rather than the real presence of God. She was no doubt convinced in her own mind that she was correct. After all, her father King Saul had never needed the Ark in his kingdom, so why did David? She criticised and despised this new move of God to her own loss.

Whilst Michal's attitude was self-righteous and counter-productive it is, nevertheless, very similar to positions adopted by many churches today. Instead of rejoicing in their position as Bride to the king, they choose to invest much of their time criticizing and looking down on new things that God is doing in other churches. Michal could have been leading the worship with her husband, showing the younger girls how to praise the LORD, but she preferred to remain aloof and considered herself too good for this new form of celebration. Despite Michal's opinion that this worship style was unnecessarily over the top, it was something new that God was doing.

David knew God's presence was real and he was not going to stop his dancing, worship and praise. Michal was going to miss out on the new blessing that God was bringing to his people. Sadly, because of her cold-hearted condition, 'Michal ... had no children to the day of her death.'[272] Her barrenness could have been because her bridegroom would never be intimate with her again due to her negative attitude. A church that adopts Michal's poor example will suffer the same fate of barrenness in their lives, having no fruit or increase. Despite having a privileged royal position, such a church will fail to be blessed and will not grow. A bride in this condition, just like Michal, will have nothing to pass onto the next generation.

Abishag
The Coming Royal Bride.

1 Kings 1:3-4 'They searched throughout Israel for a beautiful girl and found Abishag, a Shunammite, and brought her to the king. The girl was very beautiful; she took care of the king and waited on him, but the king had no intimate relations with her.'

In Scripture, Shunammite women are a picture of the unsurpassed beauty of God's ideal Bride. Whether it is the Shunammite who cared for Elisha and received a resurrected son[273] or the object of Solomon's desire in the Song of Songs,[274] these ladies are praised for their faith and loveliness. They are portrayed as a model bride fit for a king. Abishag the Shunammite combined the rare qualities of humility and beauty in a single person. She was brought into the presence of King David and served him. She did not, however, become united with him in marriage because she is a picture of the future royal Bride.

---

272   2 Sam. 6:23
273   2 Kings 4:8
274   Song of Songs 6:13 (Shulammite can be a variant of Shunammite)

Abishag represents the Bride who is yet to come. She will be given to the coming 'Son of David' the king who will rule in the coming 'Golden Kingdom' when the temple will be established and God will dwell with men. Abishag is a powerful picture of the church that Jesus is coming for. Solomon would take Abishag as his bride and she would belong to him. Solomon understood the importance of the bride's position in establishing his kingdom.

10

The Wisdom of the Bride

'Solomon answered…"Why do you request Abishag the Shunammite
for Adonijah? You might as well request the kingdom for him!"'
1 Kings 2:22

Solomon was wise. Upon being established as the new king, and through his wisdom, he knew one fact was essential above all others in securing his throne: whoever possessed the Royal Bride controlled the Kingdom. Solomon had observed that his older brothers had all forfeited their rights to the throne, with each of them having one specific fault in common. They had all failed to respect the importance of the Royal Brides. Amnon raped the king's daughter,[275] Adonijah tried to steal the king's bride,[276] and Absalom slept with the king's concubines.[277] Abuse of the royal bride resulted in loss of the kingdom, even to a son of the king. The Bride and the kingdom must not be separated in the understanding of Solomon; he must respect and possess both. Satan knows this too and that is why he continually seeks to take 'The Woman' for himself. The devil wants his

275   2 Sam. 13:10-14
276   1 Kings 2:13-17
277   2 Sam. 16:22

kingdom and his seed to prevail, but God will never allow it to happen. It is the seed of the woman that prevails over the serpent and it is the Bride of Christ who will reign with Jesus in his kingdom. A kingdom without the bride is an empty and fruitless inheritance. It is only the treasure hidden in the field that gives real value to the land,[278] and the Bride is Christ's greatest treasure. Jesus did not die to obtain land and property, He had already created everything and could easily recreate a new heaven and a new earth; he died to redeem his Bride. He shed his blood to purchase the thing that his heart loved above all others, the most precious thing in creation, his Bride. He betrothed himself to her to ensure that no one else had a legal right to take her. He will reign in his kingdom with his Bride at his side, and together 'they will reign for ever and ever.'[279]

> *'whoever possessed the Royal Bride, controlled the kingdom.'*

Solomon understood the mystery of the Bride. He grasped her essential nature and knew that nothing was more important to the success of his kingdom than respecting and possessing the Royal Bride. He would make sure that Abishag the Shunammite belonged to him. He would also make sure that anyone who dared to take her for themselves would pay with their lives. Solomon's wisdom on the true nature of the Bride of Christ is very profound. He knew that God had created man and woman to reign together[280] and he perceived that 'in the Lord, woman is not independent

---

278   Matt. 13:44
279   Rev. 22:5
280   Gen. 1:28

of man, nor is man independent of woman.'[281] Solomon's writings all contain a fascination with the mystery of the Bride, and therefore help to give a correct understanding of the essential character and purpose of the church that God is searching for.

Solomon's Wisdom on Women

1 Kings 4:29 'God gave Solomon wisdom and very great insight, and a breadth of understanding as measureless as the sand on the seashore.'

The 'Wisdom of Solomon' is well acknowledged in the Bible. Solomon asked God for wisdom and God answered his request. What many people miss, however, is that Solomon's greatest wisdom was observed in his seeking to understand the nature of the 'woman.' God's greatest gift to Solomon was in granting him the ability to comprehend the importance of the Bride. Solomon sought to obtain greater revelation as to what she represented as the essential component of the kingdom, and the perfect partner for the king. Solomon spent most of his life searching for the perfect royal bride and it could be said that he failed in his attempt. Only Jesus has succeeded in finding the perfect woman through his church. Solomon married hundreds of women hoping that one of them would prove to be the perfect one, but his writings lead to the conclusion that he never found the ideal bride. The epilogue of the book of proverbs starts with the exasperated cry; 'a wife of noble character who can find?'[282] Solomon does, however, provide the church with very valuable information concerning the true Bride's condition and relationship to

---

281   1 Cor. 11:11
282   Prov. 31:10

the king. The first display of Solomon's wisdom was seen in ensuring that the Shunammite only belonged to him and that any other man who attempted to take her would be executed. The church's primarily foundation is always grasping that it belongs to Christ, and only to him. Satan's claims on the Bride were cancelled out on the cross once and for all. Having established ownership of his Bride, some other aspects of Solomon's wisdom on her elusive nature can be examined.

Bride of Flesh or Spirit?

1 Kings 3:27 'Then the king gave this ruling: "Give the living baby to the first woman. Do not kill him; she is the mother."'

Solomon's wisdom was also revealed in how he identified and separated the two different natures of the woman. When the two prostitutes were brought before Solomon, his wise ruling revealed a true understanding of the heart and nature of a good woman. It is interesting that he knew both women were prostitutes, but he did not condemn either of them for this. He also knew that both woman did not have a husband and were fighting amongst themselves, but he did not instruct them how to reform their lives or improve their behaviour. Instead he cut straight to the real nature of the heart condition of the women; when ordering that the baby be cut in two the true inner character of each woman would be revealed.

When Christ deals with his Bride he uses a similar procedure to Solomon. Jesus does not judge believers according to the outward immoral conduct of their previous 'unmarried' life, neither does he command people to merely obey the law and live a reformed lifestyle. He does something fundamentally drastic to the situation in wielding the 'sword of his word'[283] to cut into the heart and reveal the very nature of a person's heart and soul. The two prostitutes represent the two very different natures of believers. One nature is lying and vindictive, willing to kill, steal and destroy. This carnal woman was content to allow the baby to die in order to satisfy her selfish malice. The other woman had a completely different nature. She operated from a heart of love and recognised that the life of another soul was more important than her own satisfaction. She was willing to sacrifice her own rights in order to protect the life of another. She knew that 'the Spirit gives life and the flesh counts for nothing.'[284] She was the real mother and the king could see it.

The real Bride of Christ has the same nature as the second woman. She is of the Spirit and not the flesh. She has received the nature of her Bridegroom who was willing to give his life to save others. To the casual observer the two women may look the same outwardly, but the wise Bridegroom looks at the heart and always recognises the difference between a prostitute and his potential Bride. Like this woman the church exists to give its life in ransom for others. The Bride does that which gives life to others, no matter what the cost to her own self. She knows that the wise King always sees the truth and he will ensure that 'whoever loses their life will preserve it.'[285]

---

283   Heb. 4:12
284   John 6:63
285   Luke 17:33

The Bride's Palace

1 Kings 7:8 'Solomon also made a palace...for pharaoh's daughter, whom he had married.'

Solomon's wisdom dictated that the things important to the establishment of his own kingdom must also have vast buildings to consolidate his government and rule. The valuable things in his kingdom must have dwellings in which to reside. Solomon embarked upon an unsurpassed national building programme, which took a long time to be completed. The most important building in Israel was the construction of Solomon's temple that would be inhabited by the presence of God. Nothing was more essential to Solomon than ensuring that the presence of God resided in Jerusalem. He also built his palace called the 'Forest of Lebanon,'[286] where the kings of the earth would be granted an audience with the ruler of Israel. The king must have a place to live or there can be no prestige to his kingdom. What many people overlook, is that Solomon also made sure that there was a palace for his royal bride incorporated as part of his own residence.

The Bible gives extensive details concerning the importance of these buildings, but it is not possible to explore them in great detail here. What is essential, is that the church grasps that Christ is also constructing a palace for his Bride. It may appear to have taken a very long time to be finished and the Bride may become impatient waiting for her new home to be completed, but it will soon be time for her to move in. Solomon's bride – despite her long and patient wait of around thirteen years[287] –

---

286   1 Kings 7:2
287   1 Kings 7:1

knew she needed to be ready to leave Egypt and relocate to her new palace.

Jesus informed his disciples that he was going to the Father's house 'to prepare a place for them.'[288] He let the church know that he would build a house for his Bride. He also promised to come back and take her to be with him.[289] Jesus will indeed take his church away from her earthly home to her heavenly residence. The timing of this 'taking away' is not known. What can be assumed is that just as Ezekiel's bride was 'taken away' prior to the temple's destruction,[290] Christ's Bride will also be taken to her dwelling before the judgement on this world. The Bride is to be 'snatched away' before God's wrath is poured out. It is not the Church's destiny to suffer God's wrath.[291]

The Bride Yet to Come?

Luke 11:31 'The Queen of the South came from the utmost parts of the earth to hear the wisdom of Solomon; and behold something greater than Solomon is here.'

Solomon was wise enough to understand that he was not the perfect king, and so he had no right to expect to obtain the perfect bride. In obtaining so many wives, he certainly had exerted a great deal of effort in attempting to get her. Despite Solomon's limitations, his life does provide the church with a good parable of God's bridegroom and his Bride. Just as Solomon obtained women from many nations to belong to him, so the Bride of

---

288   John 14:2
289   John 14:3
290   Ezek. 24:16
291   1 Thess. 5:9

Christ is made up of people from every nation.

Although Solomon had seven hundred wives, most biblical information on the royal queens in his life is reserved for one woman in particular. The great mystery is that this woman did not even become his bride, but it is hard to believe that this man who 'loved many foreign women'[292] did not have at least some flame of desire for her. Even in the Psalm he wrote, Solomon hints at his desire for the things of Sheba.[293] The Queen of Sheba is a very mysterious figure in scripture, but this should come as no surprise as the coming Bride is always shrouded in mystery throughout the Bible. The Queen of Sheba points towards the future royal Bride, the one that is yet to come. God's concern with the future Queen of the South is emphasised again in the book of Acts.[294] He had predestined that a beautiful church would one day arise out of Africa.

Solomon was certainly not perfect; he was just a shadow of the true 'Son of David' that would reign over God's eternal kingdom. The Queen of Sheba is only a picture of the future Bride of Christ who would be given to him in a coming marriage. Although she would be overwhelmed with his kingdom and amazed by his wisdom, Solomon could not have this bride, she eluded him and remained beyond his grasp. As a foreshadow of the church, she was reserved for a future day when a Bridegroom greater than Solomon would appear. When that future King revealed himself, the queen would be given to him as the perfect royal Bride.

---

292   1 kings 11:1
293   Psalm 72:15 (a psalm of Solomon)
294   Acts 8:27

Solomon's Search for the Bride

Prov. 18:22 'He who finds a wife finds what is good and receives favour from the LORD.'

Contrary to what many people believe, the proverbs of Solomon are not merely snippets of good advice to help on the journey of life. A closer examination of this book of wisdom reveals a hidden longing in the king's heart and points to a deep mystery. An intimate study of it illuminates an unravelling of something 'too amazing... [to] understand...the way of a man with a maiden.'[295]

Women are described throughout Proverbs and it gives essential advice and speaks abundantly about Solomon's search for the perfect bride. The book details the inner character and desirable attributes of the true woman of God. Solomon begins the book by explaining its purpose of attaining, acquiring and understanding wisdom. In the first few chapters, however, he makes it very clear that the wisdom the king is looking for is to be found in the imagery of a woman. By the end of the book the search for the 'Noble Bride' reaches a dramatic climax, as the writer's heart is laid bare in expressing his idea of a perfect wife.

It appears that, despite having hundreds of wives, Solomon was continually searching for the ideal bride. When reading the book of Proverbs from this standpoint, it gives additional information on the Bride after God's own heart, a picture of the church he is searching for.

Proverbs teaches much about 'wisdom', but it is often described as a woman. 'She will protect...she will watch over...she will exalt and she

---

295   Prov. 30:18-19

will honour.'[296] Solomon's proverbs give a vast amount of detail about the nature of this woman called wisdom. Amongst other things, 'she builds her house...prepares her table...and calls out to the lost.'[297]

Prov. 31:10 'A wife of noble character who can find?'

At the end of the book the epilogue gives the conclusion to the author's search for wisdom. The summing up of this wisdom reminds everyone once again of God's greatest thought. This wisdom of the divine mind is displayed in finding a Bride for his Son, and Proverbs chapter 31 is a picture of the church that God seeks. The detail concerning this woman is vast, but in summary: she is valued above the most expensive jewels and her husband is fully confident in her; she performs good deeds, works hard with her hands and provides for her family; she is strong, fruitful and generous to the poor and needy; she has no fear and is given great respect and dignity; she is wise, faithful and productive; and she is blessed by people and praised and rewarded by God.[298]

When reading this final chapter of Proverbs the reader will see the direct similarities between the action of this bride and many activities described in Jesus' parables. She provides servants with food, buys a field, plants a vineyard, trades profitably, works at night, keeps watch, shares her possessions, speaks well of others and keeps her lamp lit. She is not only a picture of Solomon's ideal wife, she is also a portrait of the Bride that Jesus is searching for in the Gospels. She is the model of the perfect church and a picture of the Bride of Christ. 'Many women do noble

---

296   Prov. 4:6-8
297   Prov. 9:1-6
298   Prov. 31:10-31

things but you surpass them all.'[299]

The book of Proverbs is also concerned with painting a picture of the false bride that also exists. This deceptive woman entices the foolish and is to be avoided. Solomon is very clear in warning people against the 'wayward wife with her seductive words, who has left the partner of her youth and ignored the covenant she made before God.'[300] This unfaithful bride is called an 'adulterous,'[301] 'immoral,'[302] 'prostitute'[303] who preys upon the lives of others.

Much is said concerning this failed bride, because God is aware that many people are deceived after their original commitment to Christ and turn away from him to lead lives of immorality. Worse still is the sad fact that many churches have turned away from devotion to their Saviour to follow the ways of the world. Solomon labels this type of false religion as 'folly' despite its loudness, prestige and high profile.[304] Many are attracted to this type of 'pseudo spirituality' 'but little do they know that the dead are there and that her guests are in the depths of the grave.'[305] The reality of the existence and temptations of the adulterous bride – the false church – are evident throughout the Bible.

Solomon understood the mystery of the Bride and had probably married some women who were false wives. Through his wisdom, however, it can be seen that the King's greatest search was to obtain the perfect bride. Even in the book of Ecclesiastes where the vanity of life is described,

299	Prov. 31:29
300	Prov. 2:16-17
301	Prov. 5:3
302	Prov. 6:24
303	Prov. 7:10
304	Prov. 9:13-16
305	Prov. 9:18

Solomon advises the reader to 'enjoy life with your wife, whom you love, all the days of this meaningless life.'[306] He knew that his enjoyment of life could only be found with the ideal wife that he loved. That ideal life for the Bride would only be achieved when the perfect husband appeared to take her away with him to eternal life. Solomon sought to help people understand this and that is why he encapsulated the mystery of the Bride through a song; the Song of Songs.

Solomon's Song of the Bride

Song of Songs 5:16 'He is altogether lovely. This is my beloved and this is my friend.'

Just as Jesus is 'King of Kings and Lord of Lords', so Solomon's 'Song of Songs' is the greatest of all ballads. This song is the poetic revelation of the love relationship between the bride and the groom. It is the story, in song, of the greatest romance in history. It is the prophetic story of God's search for his Bride and her response to his serenade of love. Through his wisdom, Solomon understood that some people are more likely to listen to a message in song rather than read a written document. Because of this insight he hid the message of God's love for his Bride in poetry. His hope was that she could listen to her bridegroom's song and her ears could be opened to the full nature of their relationship. The depths of the full nature of the Song cannot be encompassed in this book, but an overview may help to give an appreciation and a broader understanding.

The song would begin with the early passion of a love relationship, then grow and develop into the blossoming beauty of a mature and perfect

---

306   Eccl. 9:9

love. The bride would enter the relationship by being overwhelmed by the presence of the bridegroom stating 'your love is more delightful than wine.'[307] She quickly declares, 'take me away with you – let us hurry! Let the king bring me into his chambers.'[308] The bridegroom responds by reminding her over and over again how pleased he is with her and confesses 'how beautiful you are, my darling! Oh, how beautiful!'[309] Such is the beginning of the relationship between Christ and his church. The Song describes the growing nature of the relationship and gives deep illumination of the richness of the love between the two partners.

The motives of the bridegroom in the Song are quite clear. He desires his betrothed bride to be dressed and ready for when he comes to take her away. He comes in the night at an hour when she does not expect him. There appear to be two different dreams of the bride in this song with separate responses and different outcomes. In the first instance the bride finds her lover in the night, does not let him go, and is taken away by him to the mountains.[310] She knows and testifies that 'I am my beloved's, and my beloved is mine.'[311] In the second example the bride is awaked from sleep when she declares 'Listen! My lover is knocking: "Open to me, my sister, my darling, my dove, my flawless one."'[312] Unfortunately, this bride is not ready and she does not get dressed or open the door for him. He tries to grab her but she is out of reach and is left behind when he departs. She suffers beating and bruising from the watchmen as she

---

307   Song of Songs 1:1
308   Song of Songs 1:4
309   Song of Songs 1:15
310   Song of Songs 3 and 4
311   Song of Songs 6:3
312   Song of Songs 5:2

attempts to find her bridegroom.

The song describes the history and unfolding destiny for God's people. It is an essential prophetic parable for the Bride of Christ to take to heart. The church must get ready for the coming of her Bridegroom. She must respond to his love and his instructions or she may risk being left behind. Many Christians waste valuable energy arguing theological specifics regarding the timing of the rapture and the second coming of Jesus. The true Bride is so in love with her Bridegroom that she does not allow herself to be distracted from the preparations that are required to ensure she is ready when he arrives. She knows he is coming for her, even in the night,[313] and that is of primary importance. She will be taken by him to belong to him for ever. Even the 'friends' in the song understand this and are seen to observe the bride 'coming up from the desert leaning on her lover.'[314]

The Song concludes with the bridegroom calling to all those who will hear. The bride has ears to hear and responds with the declaration, 'come away, my lover…on the spice laden mountains.'[315] Throughout the song, Solomon is revealing the purpose of the Bride and her future destiny with the groom. When reading this song, believers can envisage a fuller understanding of the nature of their beginning and ending in Christ. The church must be in love with Jesus and this desire must intoxicate every area of their life. Lukewarm love is useless in the relationship. The Bride must not risk being unprepared, unwashed or unclothed. Jesus warned that some would not be ready and would not open the door when he

---

313   1 Thess. 5:2
314   Song of Songs 8:5
315   Song of Songs 8:14

knocks.[316] He gave many warnings, even to people close to him, and these instructions could not have been without purpose. He said that some of the people invited to the wedding would be shut outside because they did not get ready.[317] Every word of Jesus had meaning and all who follow him must take these words to heart. The true Bride is fully in love with Christ and is ready and waiting for her Bridegroom's return, to be taken to the banqueting table.

316   Rev. 3:20
317   Mat. 25:1-13

11

The Bride at the Table

'He has brought me to his banqueting table
and his banner over me is love.'
Song of Songs 2:4 (KJV)

God has called his Bride to join him at his table. Jesus often stressed the importance of the coming wedding supper where his Bride would sit at his side. He made clear that all were invited to this great banquet and that his church should endeavour to persuade everyone to get ready to attend this coming event. It was whilst at the table that Jesus instructed his people to remember him through the breaking of bread. The Lord's Table is a very important picture in scripture. All God's people are instructed to remember him through the bread and wine of communion at his table. The faithful church does this regularly, looking forward to the day when she will be at the feast, drinking and eating at the table of her Bridegroom. Women often approached Jesus whilst he was at the table and they could be taken as a type of Bride that he accepts. God's word gives careful guidance about the attitude that the church should have in approaching his table.

The Sinful Woman

Luke 7:36-38 'Jesus...reclined at the table. When a woman who had lived a sinful life in that town learned that Jesus was eating at the Pharisee's house, she stood behind him at his feet, weeping, she began to wet his feet with her tears. Then she wiped them with her hair, kissed them and poured perfume on them.'

Before anyone can be accepted by Christ they must first know and accept that they are sinful in comparison to God's holy standard. All have sinned in life and no one is righteous before God.[318] Failure to acknowledge this truth prohibits anyone receiving grace at God's table. Whether the sin is well known, as in the case of this woman, or well hidden, like many people of today, God sees everyone's sin and it is all unacceptable to him. Despite her publicly known sin, this woman came to Jesus at the table and in doing so knew that other people would condemn her. They would point out her sinful faults and may even be disgusted at the thought that she would dare to touch Jesus. Although fully aware of her own sins and the judgement and opinions of the other people in the town, she still came to Jesus at the table.

She Stood

She knew she did not deserve to be there and she completely accepted that there would be no seat reserved for her at this feast, but she still stood there nonetheless. Through simple faith she believed that the man at the table was different than all the other men she had ever known. By standing and not sitting she attracted attention, which allowed others an

---

318   Rom. 3:10

opportunity to acknowledge her sin and discuss her unworthiness. Her faith drove her past this shame and enabled her to stand in the hope that Jesus would forgive her sin. Her tears were an authentic sign of her inner-heart condition. True inner repentance is often accompanied with tears, and

> *'When a woman weeps, God always sees.'*

when a woman weeps God always sees.[319] Her simple but genuine faith in coming to Jesus at the table would transform her from a sinful lady to a woman of God whose sins were forgiven. It was at the table that she would demonstrate her full appreciation of her Lord and it was at the table that Jesus publically declared that her sins were forgiven and her faith had saved her.[320]

She Worshipped

As this woman stood there weeping, she did three things at the feet of Jesus. Firstly, she wiped his feet with her hair. A woman's hair is her covering,[321] given as a representation of the glory bestowed upon her by God. Some women who were chosen to be brides in the Old Testament had their hair shaved in order for their old identity to be removed, so that the new hair – the glory for her new bridegroom – could increase. [322]This woman used her hair as a public demonstration that she was willing to give all her glory to Jesus. She was not putting on a performance for the other people at the table; she was humbly acknowledging that all

---

319   John 20:15
320   Luke 7:48-50
321   1 Cor. 11:15
322   Deut. 21:11-13

glory belonged to Jesus. Likewise, it is only when the church stops its performance and is ready to ascribe all its glory to Jesus that it is entering into true worship.

Secondly, she kissed his feet. The most common Greek word for worship in the New Testament is 'proskuneo' which can be interpreted as to 'come towards and kiss.' This woman was worshipping Jesus in the simplest way she understood. No doubt she was aware that some people present would express their opinion that her public display of affection was inappropriate or even vulgar. True worship is often despised by people who have no love relationship with the Lord. Jesus, however, received it just as he always accepts real worship from his church. There was no music and no liturgy, only hostility and angry looks from religious hypocrites. But the woman worshipped Jesus who was pleased with her faith and accepted her.

Thirdly, she poured perfume on his feet. In the Bible oil and perfume are symbols of the Holy Spirit. When the church worships her Lord in Spirit and truth, she is becoming the Bride that he has always been seeking. True worship is always in Spirit and in truth, as Jesus informed the Samaritan woman, and that is the kind of worship that God seeks.[323] Whilst the Pharisees looked on in contempt, this sinful woman was providing Jesus with what he had always desired. She did what the church is called to do. She worshipped correctly at the Lords table, which resulted in peace, salvation and forgiveness being given to her. The Bride of Christ follows her example.

---

323   John 4:23

The Canaanite Woman

Matt. 15:22 'A Canaanite woman came to him crying out, "Lord, Son of David, have mercy on me!"

Matt. 15:27 'She said, "but even the dogs eat the crumbs that fall from their masters' table."

This Canaanite woman came to Jesus with faith, as she had grasped some understanding of what is available from the master's table. Unfortunately, many members of the church today behave more like the Corinthian believers in their recognition and understanding of the Lord's Table,[324] rather than following the example of this Canaanite lady. She was well aware that much in her life should cancel out any prospect of receiving anything from God, but she had expectant faith in the grace of God nonetheless.

The most obvious barrier preventing her from receiving grace was her nationality, Canaanite. Other Gospel writers provide additional details that would support her obvious exclusion: she lived in Tyre and 'The woman was a Greek, born in Syrian Phoenicia.'[325] No wonder the disciples asked Jesus to send her away, this woman appeared to represent everything that the Jewish Messiah wanted to get rid of. The Canaanites and the Greeks had done their best to destroy the culture and religion of Israel, so surely the last thing Jesus desired in his kingdom was a woman who represented these destructive false beliefs. She really did not fit in with their understanding of acceptability. Many in the church today also feel that they are outsiders who do not fit into the mould of

---

324   1 Cor. 11:17-32
325   Mark 7:26

acceptable religion. Nevertheless, like this woman they have not come to the disciples, they have come to Jesus at his table and he does not send them away.

She Knelt

Matt. 15:25 'The woman came and knelt before him. "Lord, help me!" she said.

It is interesting to note that at her first cry for mercy Jesus gave her no answer. Jesus spoke only to the disciples and indicated that he was only sent to the Israelites not the Canaanites. This may have been because her declaration that he was the Son of David pointed only to his status as the Jewish Messiah and not a Canaanite Saviour. Jesus may have paused in silence to enable her to rethink her approach to him and grasp that he was much more than just the King of Israel. Alternatively, it may simply have been a way of testing the sincerity of her faith. Silence from God does not necessarily mean he is not listening.

Whatever the reason, she was determined to get close to Jesus. It could have been that she had heard the ancient stories of another Canaanite woman who had lived over a thousand years before her.[326] Perhaps she knew how Rahab and her family were saved by a previous 'Joshua'[327] and how she had been transformed from a prostitute into a bride. Driven by some inner passion she pressed forward towards Jesus; somehow perceiving that this man never turned away a woman of faith.

Having received no verbal answer from Jesus she knelt before him.

---

326   Josh. 6:25
327   'Joshua' is the Hebrew for the Greek name 'Jesus'

Receiving no initial answer from God does not mean that he has said no. It may simply imply that he is waiting for you to kneel. Kneeling often indicates that a person is adopting a position of submission, prayer, and patient waiting. So often the church shouts out requests to the Lord but less seldom does it kneel, submit and patiently pray. There is great power in kneeling before the Lord. This is not to get his attention, he already sees everything, but more so He can get someone's full attention.

This woman had a great need, but before her petition could be granted Jesus required her to understand who he really was. He was not just a religious leader of the Jews; he was the Lord of all nations on Earth. He was the heavenly Bridegroom who had come to seek his Bride. It is only by kneeling in submission and giving recognition to who Jesus really is, that the church is correctly placed and ready to receive from his table.

Even as she knelt before him, Jesus continued to test her faith in order to increase her understanding of the nature of her relationship to him. It may appear quite shocking that Jesus stated that 'dogs' had no right to eat from his table. In receiving this kind of response, many believers of today would have taken offense and departed. Many can put up with opposition from other disciples and may remain faithful during apparent unanswered prayer, but when the Pastor calls them a dog it's time to leave. This woman, however, knew by faith that there was provision at the master's table, despite all other surrounding influences. She was not going to allow offense to enter her heart and she was determined to obtain the grace and mercy in her time of need.[328]

In a similar way, believers today must never allow offense to become a

---

328   Heb. 4:16

stumbling block in their lives. The true Bride of Christ remains faithful to her master's table, even through external difficulties, because she knows that the 'testing of [her] faith develops perseverance.'[329] She will persevere because even the lowest of dogs can still eat crumbs from his table. When the final test had been passed the woman's request was granted. Her faith in the grace of God found at the Lord's Table provided healing for her family. Likewise, as the church kneels is submission to eat the bread from the Lord's Table, his healing power is supplied regardless of the historic background of his Bride.

Esther

Esther 2:17-18 'He set a royal crown on her head and made her queen instead of Vashti. And the king gave a great banquet, Esther's banquet.'

Here again the Bible provides a clear picture of the bride at the table. Before Esther is considered, it is important to note exactly who she was and what kind of bride she was called to be. Esther was a replacement bride for a previous queen, Vashti. The king had originally called her to his banquet table, but at 'the Kings command, Queen Vashti refused to come.'[330] The result of this disobedience was that Vashti was banished from the king's presence forever and the king would now look for another bride.

The story of Esther is a miniature summary of the greater story of God's Bride. Vashti, just like Eve, disobeyed God's original call, lost her position and was banished from the place God had provided for her. Thankfully,

---

329   James 1:3
330   Esther 1:12

in his mercy, God did not withdraw his love for mankind when Eve was deceived. On the contrary, he put into operation the greatest rescue plan that creation had ever witnessed. The Son of God would still obtain a Bride, one who would join him at the banquet table. Eve and Vashti may have failed, but Esther would overcome by faith; she represents the restored Bride of Christ.

The focus in the book of Esther is specifically on the Bride; God's name is never even mentioned. Through this wonderful book God is revealing very important aspects concerning the nature of his Bride, the mystery that is often hidden away.

Esther had two names. Esther was her gentile name, but her original name was the Jewish 'Hadassah'. The church must always remember that her origins come from Israel and it is only through being grafted into God's promises to the Jews that the church has her position. The church does not replace Israel; God's Bride always includes both Jew and Gentile.[331]

Also, Esther had three people guiding and protecting her life. These were; her bridegroom the king; her adopted father Mordecai; and the hidden servant in the harem. In the same way, the church has three divine protectors and guides: Jesus the Bridegroom; The Heavenly Father; and the hidden Holy Spirit.

The eunuch of the harem would provide Esther with gifts and pour perfume on her in preparation for her wedding banquet. In the same way, the Holy Spirit makes the church ready to meet Jesus. He distributes his gifts and clothes the church in perfumed garments ready to be taken to the table with Jesus. Just as Esther's Bridegroom and king accepts her into

---

331   Gal. 3:28

his presence and promises her all that is his, so Jesus awaits the church to come to his table and share in his great inheritance. Mordecai adopted Esther into his family and guided her every day so that 'she continued to follow Mordecai's instructions, as she had done when he was bringing her up.'[332] Similarly, the Heavenly Father adopts believers into his family and gives them daily advice, care and provision. Esther obeyed all these three men in her life and the result of her obedience was success and salvation for her people. When the church fully obeys everything that her Heavenly Bridegroom, Father, and Counsellor advise, she too will fulfil her destiny like Esther and become the Bride God always desired.

Esther Reclined

Esther 7:8 'Esther was reclining.'

Esther was not just a bride; she was also the queen and the most beloved woman in the kingdom. She was not permitted to kneel or stand at the table, she was obligated to recline as her royal position dictated. Esther could afford to be secure and confident in the knowledge of who she was. She could rest in the presence of her bridegroom, as she knew that no one could harm her while she dined with her husband the king. She had a respectful fear of the king, but she was afraid of no other man.

After Esther had obtained her position at the Kings table, she was obliged to act in accordance with Mordecai's instructions and fulfil her destiny. She had 'come to royal position for such a time as this.'[333] Even when she had obtained her position at the table, Esther still had a job to do and so

---

332   Esther 2:20
333   Esther 4:14

does the church. God's purpose for his Bride is not that she merely 'gets saved' and then lounges about reclining in the presence of the Lord. Once she is established in her royal place at the table, the church must utilise her favoured position to speak to the king. She must persuade the king to carry out the necessary righteous actions to protect her people.

Despite Esther's apparent safety, Haman, the enemy of the Jews, had devised a plot to annihilate the children of Abraham. He thought his despicable plan was sure to succeed and his pride led him to be overconfident in his wicked scheme to kill, steal and destroy. Indeed, the plot may have succeeded if God had not used his secret weapon to protect his people. God's ultimate deterrent to combat Satan's power was Esther, the hidden bride of the king. Haman would soon discover the real power of the Bride at the table and he would be destroyed as a result. Just as the king and Esther had authority, so the church must recognise that all authority has been given to Jesus Christ and that he shares his authority with his Bride.[334]

Esther 5:4 '"If it pleases the king," replied Esther, "Let the king, together with Haman, come today to a banquet I have prepared for him."

Esther understands that she cannot defeat Haman in her own strength. She knows how manipulative he is and is fully aware of his schemes, but she also realises that there is a way to defeat him. Her plan was to bring him to the king's table. If her enemy's plans could be brought to the attention of the king, she was confident that he would deal with the matter. She knew that the king at the table would forgive and accept her,

---

334   Matt. 28:18

and she also understood that he would protect and avenge anyone who dared to touch his Bride.

The church must also grasp the full significance of coming to the table of the Lord. It is not only a place of ceremony and remembrance, but also a place of real spiritual transformation and power. The awesome power of the king at his table must never be underestimated. Some members of the Corinthian church failed to recognise the full implications of the Lord's Table and paid with their lives.[335] Esther knew the power of her bridegroom and she was not afraid to use it against evil.

The table was set and the bread and the wine was partaken; then and only then, did Esther petition the king. She did not call for destruction or punishment of her enemy, she merely asked her husband to spare her life and the lives of her people. That is all she said, and it was enough. The king would sort out the rest.

It was at the communion table that Jesus showed the church 'the full extent of his love.'[336] When the church submits to the full provision of God's love she will find an ample supply of divine protection from the one who loved her more than life itself. When the Lord of the church hears his Bride's cry for help, his answer is swift.

Esther's bridegroom didn't need to hear any additional information, he had heard enough. Someone had dared to threaten his bride, and they would pay with their life. 'The king got up in a rage, left his wine and went out.'[337] The wine on the table represents the forgiveness for the Bride, but the wine was left when dealing with Haman. Hundreds of

---

335   1 Cor. 11:30
336   John 13:1
337   Esther 7:7

years later, another son of perdition would reject the wine of forgiveness at the table of the Lord and seek to harm the people of God. When he rejected Jesus at the table, Judas Iscariot sealed his fate. When it comes to protecting his church, Jesus ultimately acts and there will be no mercy for the Bride's enemies. Those who rejects the wine of mercy will drink the wine of His fury and wrath. [338]

Esther 7:8 'The king exclaimed, "Will he even molest the queen while she is with me in the house?"'

The king returned, and in the biblical pattern the King always returns for his bride. In the king's absence and through his innate foolishness, Haman had even dared to touch the queen as she reclined on the couch. The king's countenance spoke for itself, everyone in the palace knew that anyone who touched the queen would die. Nothing more needed to be said and Esther does not even speak or defend herself further, she knew her husband would protect her. The King's soldiers removed Haman from the table and he was hanged. All who oppose God and seek to harm his people will receive no mercy when the king returns. The church must continue to recline at the Lord's Table just like Esther. It is at the table that the Bride of Christ can be at rest knowing that she is secure under the divine protection of her Bridegroom and king.

---

338   Rev. 14:10

Mary of Bethany

John 12:3 'Mary took about a pint of pure nard, an expensive perfume; she poured it on Jesus' feet and wiped his feet with her hair.'

John 12:7 'It was intended that she should save this perfume for the day of my burial.'

Mary provided the last act of devotion for the body of Jesus before his suffering at Calvary. During the last supper Jesus washed the disciples' feet, but at this particular table Mary washed the feet of her master. Mary is a wonderful picture of the type of church that God is looking for. There are similarities between the actions of Mary here and the behaviour of the sinful woman in Luke chapter seven, but they are not the same event. Mary was not a sinful woman and she was not coming to get saved or forgiven, she already knew Jesus and had faith in him.

Here we witness Mary's greatest joy, which was always to be in the presence of her Lord. Mary was not performing this devotion to receive self-satisfaction; instead she was doing it because she hoped that it was the one thing that would bring her master the greatest joy. It has been seen how: the sinful woman stood at the Lord's table to be forgiven; the Canaanite woman knelt because she had a need; and Esther reclined to receive protection from the king. However, Mary came with the chief purpose of pleasing Jesus and satisfying him. She knew that worship is not a means to an end in itself. Perhaps she somehow grasped an aspect of the eternal mystery – that God was seeking a Bride for his son – and seized this last opportunity to lavish everything she had upon him in worship. Because she understood something of her purpose and destiny,

Jesus said her act of worship would always be remembered.[339]

Mary Sat

Luke 10:39 'Mary sat at the Lord's feet listening to what he said.'

Some of those present criticised Mary's worship under the misguided notion that Jesus was seeking service more than love and devotion. 'Why wasn't this perfume sold and the money given to the poor?'[340] This is often the cry of those whose heart loves their ministry more than their Lord. Mary was devoted to Jesus and had her priorities in the correct order. She understood that it is true worship that satisfies the heart of Jesus. Ministry should always follow worship, but must never replace it. Jesus has always been looking for a Bride, not a slave. Mary would not be distracted from her correct order of priorities by anyone. Even when her sister demanded that she get up and do something, Jesus reminded Martha that Mary had chosen something better. When the church decides to simply sit, worship and listen to Jesus, it can enter into a new revelation and deeper relationship with him. That is the procedure of how his true Bride enters into closer spiritual intimacy with him, and that is how it should continue.

When Mary worshipped Jesus, the whole 'house was filled with the fragrance of the perfume.'[341] Real worship changes the atmosphere of God's house. Like Martha, many churches try to improve things by telling people to work harder or be better organised. Other churches complain that more money should be given to their pet ministries and projects, as

---

339   Matt. 26:13
340   John 12:5
341   John 12:3

did some of the disciples. Mary's worship, however, was the quickest and simplest way to change the whole atmosphere of the house. When the Bride of Christ puts aside her worries and releases her love and worship on Jesus, the earthly dwelling begins to smell of the fragrance of heaven. Worship must never be replaced by anything. It must never be side-lined or moved quickly out of the way so that other more important activities can commence. The first love of the Bride must never be forsaken. Jesus longs for close fellowship and intimacy with his people. The Holy Spirit dwells in the church, so that incense and fragrance is always available to be released by those who seek to worship God. The church must worship now, not later.

Mary understood that this might have been her last chance to worship Jesus in this way. And it was. She always chose to sit at his feet and she had decided that she was going to adore him right to the end. Mary represents the church that never loses its first love.[342] It is a sad fact that many only come to the table for sins to be forgiven or to ask God to meet their present needs. Whilst these things are often necessary, mature believers recognise that God is ultimately seeking a Bride who worships at his table out of an undying love for her Lord. They, like Mary, will give all that they have while they have it, to make sure that Jesus is satisfied. Genuine people of God know that there is little point in saving up treasures on this earth or waiting for a more appropriate time to give all they have. They recognise that everything has to be given to Jesus right now, as he never guarantees another opportunity. There were many people at the table, some were serving, some reclining, and others complaining, but Mary

---

342   Rev. 2:4

was worshipping with all that she had. She represents the true Bride of Christ and what she has 'will not be taken away from her.'[343]

---

343   John 10:42

12

The Friends of the Bridegroom

'The friend who attends the bridegroom waits and listens for him, and is

full of joy when he hears the bridegrooms voice. That joy is mine.'

John 3:29

*T*hroughout God's story of the Bride it is evident that specific individuals have been present at her side. God ensured that trusted people helped to prepare the Bride to be ready for her coming Bridegroom. They are the friends of the Bridegroom, they accompany the Bride and they 'call her blessed.'[344] Jesus has many followers, but he only called certain individuals his friends.[345] These were special people; loyal and faithful companions who were trusted more than others. They heard the voice of God clearly, before the rest of God's people did. They understood the deep mystery of the Bride and they sought to ensure that she was equipped and ready for her coming wedding. God has had many friends throughout history, but some were specifically noted for their care and concern for the Bride. Jesus still seeks such individuals today, who will

---

344   Song of Songs 6:9
345   John 15:15

remember that his church is primarily his Bride. Any leaders who are true friends of the bridegroom will follow the examples set by those outlined in scripture.

John the Baptist

John 3:29-30 'The Bride belongs to the Bridegroom... He must become greater; I must become less.'

John the Baptist is a classic example of a friend of the bridegroom. Unlike many leaders of today, John understood that the church did not belong to him. It was not his possession and could not be used to increase his personal glory and prestige. Despite being the greatest prophet of the age,[346] John would produce no glossy brochure with his picture on every page. He knew that his ministry was to prepare the church for the one coming who was

'His ministry was to make the Bride ready for the coming of Jesus.'

greater than he. John was not interested in self-promotion or gaining a high profile reputation with the religious leaders of the world. He perceived from birth[347] that his ministry was to make the Bride ready for the coming of Jesus and none of the temptations, or threats, from the world would prevent him from fulfilling his mission.

---

346   Matt. 11:11
347   Luke 1:44

Eph. 5:25-27 'Husbands love your wives, just as Christ loved the church and gave himself up for her to make her holy, cleansing her by washing with water through the word, and to present her to himself as a radiant church.'

John knew his role was to wash the Bride, to ensure she was kept clean and holy. He would baptise all who came to the Jordan in genuine repentance, in order to prepare them for the coming Messiah. Being a true prophet, he would also wash people with his words, allowing nothing to contaminate God's Bride. His entire life was dedicated to this cause. He knew his God was holy, therefore, he would ensure that the Bride would be holy. He would forfeit the basic luxuries of life in pursuit of preparing the nation to meet its saviour. Luxurious food, comfortable clothing and opulent dwelling places would all be sacrificed for the sake of God's Bride. John never attempted to step outside of his specific calling, and he did not perform miracles,[348] or seek to obtain official position within the religious establishment. He never used his powerful anointing to gain glory for himself, knowing that the glory belonged to Christ and his Bride. His cleansing ministry did not only consist of water baptism. His preaching ministry would also defend and protect the Bride from outside pollution. Kings, Pharisees and Sadducees would quickly recoil from John's stinging words if they dared to inject their hypocritical religious venom into the people being made clean.[349] Even tax collectors and occupying enemy soldiers submitted to his prophetic authority.[350] John's ministry would succeed and a nation would be revived, due to his dedication in

---

348   John 10:41
349   Matt. 3:7
350   Luke 3:12-14

preparing the Bride for Christ's coming.

Matt. 14:3 'Herod arrested John and bound him and put him in prison because of Herodias, his brothers Philip's wife, for John had been saying to him: "It is not lawful for you to have her."'

John's zeal for the purity of the Bride meant that he was compelled to speak out when any bride was misused. It did not matter that Herod was the king; he still had no right to take another man's bride. Ironically, Herodias did not appreciate John's concern for her, in the same way that many in today's church resent the words of God's prophets, even when their rebukes are for their own protection. King Herod was furious with John, as he wanted possession of the bride to satisfy his own lusts.

Corrupt leaders in all ages usually presume that the Bride belongs to them. 'With eyes full of adultery, they never stop sinning; they seduce the unstable; they are experts in greed-an accursed brood!'[351] John knew Herodias was Philip's wife not Herod's, and he was prepared to speak out. Like Nathan before King David,[352] all true prophets remind leaders that they cannot take another man's bride for themselves. John would lose his life and suffer greatly for preaching the truth. Even the bride he tried to help hated him and demanded that he lose his head. John's end came at the hands of an unlawful bridegroom and a false bride. But it did not matter. John had completed his ministry. He knew the heavenly bridegroom had already arrived and that the true Bride had been prepared. John was a genuine friend to the bridegroom and his mission had succeeded. The

---

351   2 Pet. 2:14
352   2 Sam. 12:9

Bride was now washed and ready to be given to Jesus.

Joseph

Gen. 39:9 'My master has withheld nothing from me except you, because you are his wife.'

Few people in scripture display the upright moral character of Joseph. He was the most faithful servant in the house of his master and, because of his discipline, hard work and integrity, Potiphar put Joseph in charge of all he possessed. Due to the favour of God over Joseph's life, everything in Potiphar's house was also blessed. The day would come, however, when Joseph would be tested to see whether he was a true friend of the bridegroom. When the day of testing came, would he remain faithful in serving his master, or would he fall into temptation and take the bride for himself?

Although many ministers may serve God faithfully for many years, it is a sad fact that some fail when this particular temptation comes their way. They forget that God has blessed them in giving them so much authority and responsibility, and they can falsely assume that the Bride also belongs to them. The Bride, however, must never be used to satisfy their desires and a true friend of the bridegroom always remembers this.

Gen. 39:7 'his master's wife took notice of Joseph and said, "Come to bed with me!"'

Joseph's temptation to take Potiphar's wife was an extremely difficult trial for him to endure. It was not just a one off event, but a continuous problem. Despite the longevity of this temptation, he would not betray his master, 'and though she spoke to Joseph day after day, he refused to go to bed with her.'[353] Joseph may have had opportunity to rationalise and justify every carnal excuse for taking the bride for himself. Had not his master put 'everything he owns'[354] into his care? Did not the bride herself desire him, and would he not be giving her what she wanted and supplying her needs? In any case, he could have reasoned that no one would find out about their prohibited relationship, as it would mean certain death for both of them.

Many who seek to serve the Bride of Christ will suffer similar temptations to the one faced by Joseph. It is a sad fact that some deluded churches try to use God's servants to satisfy their own desires. Just like Potiphar's wife with Joseph, some carnal believers take notice of an individual's gifting and abilities and exhibit an unhealthy infatuation with them. 'Joseph was well-built and handsome'[355] and combined with his supernatural abilities to predict the future, he would surely have been adored by many in today's celebrity culture. He would probably have had his own TV show and high profile ministry accompanied by thousands of adoring followers. Although some of God's servants do succumb to the expectations of others and allow themselves to be adored and enthroned by some in church, the true friends of the bridegroom will never allow themselves to take Christ's place. A prophet's role is to please his master, not satisfy the carnal desires of the church. Others may call them great and admire their abilities, but they know that they are merely servants of the true Bridegroom. No minister should ever allow a church to give

---

353   Gen. 39:10
354   Gen. 39:8
355   Gen. 39:6

them the exalted place that belongs only to the husband of the Bride. God's servants should be honoured by the church, but never worshipped by anyone. That specific level of love and adoration is reserved only for the bridegroom. Joseph understood this.

Gen. 39:12 'She caught him by his cloak and said, "Come to bed with me!" But he left his cloak in her hand and ran out of the house'

Many of God's servants underestimate the persistent and persuasive power of some misguided Christians. There is a right way, and a wrong way, to love God's church. Joseph chose the correct way. Unfortunately, some carnal believers will act like Potiphar's wife and seek to enthrone their anointed leaders, but even Jesus would not allow people to make him king by force.[356] Some churches will encourage their leaders to take positions for which they were never equipped. They can flatter and compliment naïve pastors until they succumb to fulfilling their desires. They can behave like the adulteress in Proverbs who 'took hold of him and kissed him…looked for him and found him'[357] and 'with persuasive words she led him astray and seduced him with her smooth talk.'[358] Despite the temptation, Joseph would not be seduced. Neither the power and prestige, nor the opportunities presented by his position of responsibility, would cause him to take that which belonged to his master. Even when Potiphar's wife took away his garment, Joseph would rather run away than be in the same house as this seduction. Unfortunately, it is when some churches threaten to take away their garment of ministry, that some

---

356   John 6:15
357   Prov. 7:13-15
358   Prov. 7:21

pastors capitulate and fulfil their desires. Joseph would rather lose his ministry than betray his master and do 'such a wicked thing and sin against God.'[359] He would indeed lose his present ministry in Potiphar's house, but the loss of Joseph would mean the removal of God's blessing over the household. True prophets are not honoured in their own household[360] and seldom fully appreciated by those they serve. It is usually only after their departure that they regret the prophet's absence. Even Potiphar's bride failed to see that Joseph was actually protecting her future despite her own carnality and false accusations. Genuine friends of the Bridegroom, however, will endeavour to protect the Bride, even when she betrays them and rejects their ministry. The Heavenly Bridegroom, however, knows who his true friends are. He sees their service to his Bride, understands their sacrifice and will reward them.

Paul

2 Cor. 11:2 'I am jealous for you with a Godly jealousy. I promised you to one husband, to Christ, so that I might present you as a pure virgin to Him.'

Few individuals in history have loved the church as ardently as the apostle Paul. He grasped the mystery, perhaps more than anyone else, that the church was the Bride of Christ.[361] His love for Christ's Bride was displayed through every aspect of his life. Nothing was too great a sacrifice for Paul when it concerned the well-being of the church. He was

---

359   Gen. 39:9
360   Mark. 6:4
361   Eph. 5:32

even content to forego the right of having his own wife[362] in providing service to God's Bride. His comforts were forsaken and hardships embraced, as he faced death on a daily basis, in pursuit of presenting a pure Bride ready for her one true husband. His exploits on behalf of the church, as recorded in the book of Acts, are too numerous to be detailed here. His many letters of love to the churches are likewise too profound to be examined in this short overview of his life. One thing, however, is abundantly clear: Paul was a true friend of the Bridegroom and nothing would prevent him from serving and protecting the church with every fibre of his being.

2 Cor. 11:23 'I have worked much harder, been in prison more frequently, been flogged more severely, and been exposed to death again and again.' Paul's sufferings for the church are well noted, but what is often overlooked is the fact that his primary aim was to provide for the church, rather than to take from it. In an age where it was commonplace to allow women to do most of the menial duties work in a home, Paul would rather work with his own hands instead of being a burden to God's Bride. In contrast to Paul's example, many modern leaders expect God's Bride to perform all the work and falsely assume she exists to provide them with a comfortable and easy life. Paul could boast that, despite being in financial need, he 'was not a burden to anyone' and that 'I have kept myself from being a burden'[363] to the church. This is in sharp contrast to many pastors currently serving the church who demand to maximise

---

362   1 Cor. 9:5
363   2 Cor. 11:9

their salary before accepting any ministry position. Unfortunately, some people today have already ignored Paul's warning, corrupted their minds, and been robbed of the truth in viewing ministry as a means of financial gain.[364] Whilst recognising the fact that ministers have a right to receive financial support,[365] Paul was primarily concerned with the well-being of Christ's Bride[366] and no sacrifice was considered too much in ensuring the success of the church. He knew his reward would come with the appearance of the Bridegroom who would soon arrive.

1 Cor. 5:1 'There is sexual immorality among you.. A man has his father's wife.'

Like John the Baptist and Joseph before him, Paul's concern for the purity of Christ's Bride displayed itself in the practical application of protecting all wives, regardless to whom they belonged. Upon hearing that a bride had been taken by another man, Paul's spirit was enraged. What compounded the nature of this sin was that the woman belonged to the man's father! When sins against a bride they appear to receive a specific and severe rebuke from the friends of the Bridegroom. Paul's condemnation was clear and swift, with him instructing the church to 'Expel the wicked man from among you' and 'hand this man over to Satan'[367] The way that Paul dealt with this man's abuse of a woman provides a striking parallel to how the he dealt with anyone who misused God's Bride. His epistles were filled with attacks against 'false

---

364   1 Tim. 6:5
365   1 Cor. 9:14
366   1 Tim. 5:16
367   1 Cor. 5:5-13

apostles'[368] who attempted to appropriate God's Bride for themselves. The churches under Paul's pastoral care were repeatedly warned against 'false believers'[369] that infiltrate the fellowship and secretly seduce her with destructive heresies. These deceivers must be resisted at all costs in order to keep the Bride pure.

The church today must likewise avoid seduction by false shepherds whose real aim is to flirt with Christ's Bride, telling her what she wants to hear in order to use her for themselves. Paul warned that these manipulative leaders would abound in the final days and that 'they are the kind who worm their way into homes and gain control over weak willed women.'[370] The Lord Jesus himself warned against professional leaders who love their own self-importance whilst 'they devour widows' houses and for a show make lengthy prayers. Such men will be punished most severely.'[371] Paul had no carnal desire to use the church to satisfy his own lusts. His flesh had been dealt with on the cross where he was crucified with Christ.[372] Without the removal of their flesh, leaders are unfit and unprepared to serve Christ's Bride. All true friends of the bridegroom, however, have seen that their carnality died at Calvary and they exist to prepare the church to serve Jesus.

---

368   2 Cor. 11:13
369   Gal. 2:4
370   2 Tim. 3:6
371   Luke 20:47
372   Gal 2:20

The Eunuchs

Isaiah 56:4-5 'To the eunuchs who keep my Sabbaths, who choose what pleases me ...I will give them an everlasting name that will endure forever.'

Esther 1:10-11 'The King commanded the seven Eunuchs who served him...to bring before him queen Vashti.'

Eunuchs were a very special breed of servants. The king trusted them to take care of his most valuable and treasured possession: his bride. There was a very legitimate reason why the king placed so much trust in his eunuchs. It was because they had been altered through a painful experience and operation, which had changed their nature. The King knew that their flesh had been dealt with and that they would no longer have carnal desires concerning his bride. Their motives for serving him and his bride were pure and they could now be trusted. They are an authentic model for all ministers who desire to serve God. They represent true friends of the Bridegroom who will never use his church to satisfy their own lusts, but will endeavour to bring the Queen into the presence of the King.

The King's Eunuch

Esther 2:3 'bring all the beautiful girls into the harem...Let them be placed under the care of Hegai, the king's eunuch.'

Before Esther was taken into the king's presence she was entrusted unto the care of Hegai, a trusted eunuch of the bridegroom. His role was to make her even more beautiful than she already was, so that she would be an acceptable bride for his master. Hegai would bathe her, and provide her with special food.[373] He would also supervise her beauty treatments and lavish perfume and cosmetics on her for a whole year.[374] He would advise her how to behave and present her with gifts. No woman could have received greater attention than Esther under the care of Hegai. Despite this intimate relationship between Esther and Hegai, the eunuch was never tempted to misuse his status in taking advantage of this bride. Even as he daily viewed Esther's supreme beauty and developed a special relationship with her, he never forgot the true nature of their friendship. She did not belong to him; he was just a eunuch in the service of the king and could not provide Esther with all she required. His carnality had been removed and his fleshly desires cut off.

God cannot trust a pastor with his church if they have not first had their flesh removed.[375] Like Hegai and Esther, pastors develop a special relationship with the church that they serve. They care for her and wash her in preparation to enter the presence of the King of Kings. Nevertheless, no matter how beautiful, gifted and highly praised a church is, all of her attributes belong to God and her glory cannot be taken by anyone else. Many leaders fail to deal with their carnal natures and, after seeing how successful a church has become, they may be tempted to use its considerable attributes in satisfying themselves. God will not allow it. A leader's role, however important, is only temporary. Just as Esther left Hegai to enter the Kings presence,[376] so the church will leave this

---

373   Esth. 2:9
374   Esth. 2:12
375   Rom. 8:8
376   Esth. 2:15

earth to be with Christ. In the meantime, the Bride is being prepared for her wedding day. A true friend of the bridegroom, like Hegai, will have ensured that she has been washed, perfumed and anointed with oil before she is taken away to be with the King.

The Queen's Eunuch

Acts 8:27 'He met an Ethiopian Eunuch, an important official in charge of all the treasury of Candace, queen of the Ethiopians.'

It must not be assumed that all friends of the Bridegroom face merely sexual temptations. Being a eunuch, this unnamed African treasurer would be unlikely to enter into any physically immoral behaviour with the queen that he served. Real temptation, however, still existed to this eunuch due to the nature of his official position. A lot of money would pass through his hands and it would be very easy for him to help himself to some of it. He supervised the finances for an entire nation and no one would notice if some of it went to cover his personal expenses.

All successful churches can soon find that considerable sums of money are under their supervision and a treasurer is required to keep accounts. Not all friends of the Bridegroom are called to be preachers. It is a sad reality that, like Judas Iscariot,[377] some church stewards fails to differentiate between God's money and their own needs. The Ethiopian Treasurer could be trusted. Despite his education and important position, he still recognised his need for a minister to teach him the scriptures and he accepted that he needed salvation. So God sent Phillip to teach him the word, and he believed and was baptised and would continue on his

---

377   John 12:6

way rejoicing.[378] After his conversion, his calling would remain as the essential financial administrator to the queen. The eunuch now had a new king, but still accepted and understood that his primary ministry was to serve his queen. He would rejoice in his position, but still recognise that the Bride was not there to satisfy him, and neither were her finances. The eunuch was a true friend to this 'queen of the south'[379] and would endeavour to help her find her future King. The African church was being prepared as a Bride for Jesus, centuries before western missionaries set foot on the continent. In the fullness of time, a beautiful church would emerge out of Africa ready to serve Jesus.

Jezebel's Eunuchs

2 Kings 9:32-33 '"Who is on my side? Who?" Two or three eunuchs looked down at him. "Throw her down!" Jehu said. So they threw her down."

The friends of the Bridegroom are not only commissioned with preparing and protecting God's true Bride, they are commanded to throw down Satan's false woman. Jezebel, as shall be examined in the next chapter, is a perfect example of this false church. Everything connected with her signifies a corrupt and immoral religious system. Through her cultic charms and physical attributes she seduces all ministries under her control and manipulation. There are, however, specific individuals who cannot be tempted to succumb to her worldly beauty or political power. They are the eunuchs: those who obey the voice of the king and resist the

---

378   Acts 8:34-39
379   Luke 11:31

manipulation of a false queen. They are true servants of God who are not in bondage to their own selfish desires or attracted to the cosmetic beauty of a worldly religious system. Unlike Delilah's power over the carnal Samson, Jezebel has no power over them. They cannot be seduced and they obey the voice of God's anointed king. They hear his command to throw down the false bride, along with her heresies, and they obey his word.

In these days of rampant spiritual seduction and the proliferation of false doctrines, God is looking for his true friends today. They are ministers whose flesh has been dealt with at the cross and are spiritual eunuchs, ready to cast down all false teaching. These true servants, like Jezebel's eunuchs, have a choice to make. They either obey the voice of the true king and cast down the false queen, or submit to her control and keep their comfortable position within her kingdom. In the last days, when false religions will abound, the true friends of the Bridegroom will recognise Satan's Harlot and fulfil the command of God's true King.

13

Satan's Harlot

'The sons of God saw that the daughters of men were beautiful, and
they married any of them they chose.'
Gen. 6:2

*F*rom the beginning of creation Satan has tried to copy God's methods. For every divine conception of God, Satan produces a counterfeit. The Devil understands the essential purpose of God in creating the Bride, and he will stop at nothing in trying to obtain his own woman. Despite the divine prohibition on angelic beings being allowed to marry,[380] Satan's perversion of all things good leads him to continue to try and use women for his own means. In attempting to establish his own demonic kingdom Satan realises that he must also manufacture his own woman, someone he can manipulate for his own evil ends and use for his own satisfaction. He attempted his plan in Eden by making a move on Eve, and he has never ceased to try and make the woman dance to his tune in order to take her for himself. Satan has no love for women, only lust. He has no

---

380   Matt. 22:30

motives to fulfil her and he has no desire or capacity to give her anything of value. He merely seeks to seduce, manipulate and 'spiritually rape' Christ's Bride in order to satisfy his own diabolic ambitions.

Once the Serpent's spiritual seed had been sown into the hearts of men, Satan's tactics spread throughout the earth. By the time of Noah some of the 'Sons of God' had 'abandoned their proper dwelling'[381] and fallen into lust and pride. Sinful men and the Sons of God copied the example of Satan and attempted to take a bride for themselves. The result of this rebellion continued to increase amongst God's creation with the misuse and abuse of the woman being at the forefront of this wickedness. The fruit of this prohibited abuse was 'The Nephilim.'[382] God's condemnation and judgement was swift and, in the days of Noah, the abominable fruit of this demonic activity was destroyed in the flood.

'Satan has continued to prepare his own spiritual prostitute throughout history.'

Satan's copycat plan, however, soon restarted through the new order of life on earth. It was not long before the evil manipulator would be placing his own religious harlots in positions of power in order to bring his kingdom about on earth. Satan has continued to prepare his own spiritual prostitute throughout history hoping to coerce her into fulfilling his desires. Even during the time of Christ on earth Satan used a false queen, the immoral Herodias, to kill a friend of the bridegroom: John the

---

381   Jude 1:6
382   Gen. 6:4

Baptist, a prophet of God.[383]

Satan's counterfeit queen always opposes true believers and she detests the genuine Bride of Christ with an unbridled malice. Satan needs this woman and has persuaded her to be his slave to continue his work building a false religious system and establishing his kingdom on earth. This woman, or 'false church' will act on his behalf out of a blind and misguided obedience to his lies. All who follow Satan and his counterfeit religion will ultimately join them in their destruction. Satan's woman appears throughout earth's ages and the scriptures. She will make her most ruthless and infamous appearance alongside the Antichrist at the end of this present age. In the book of Revelation the final age of this dispensation culminates in her ultimate appearance as 'The mother of prostitutes and of the abominations of the earth.'[384]

Before examining Satan's attempt at copying the Bride, it is essential to establish an important difference between ordinary women who have sinned, and the iniquity of the 'evil harlot.' All people, including the women in scripture, have sinned. This sin does not automatically mean that they will form part of Satan's prostitute. As has been observed, many of the greatest women in the Bible had a historical record of past sins including sexual immorality and false idol worship. These women were still loved and redeemed by God and were chosen as brides through repentance and faith in Christ. For example, Hosea's wife Gomer appeared to have been habitually unfaithful, but she was eventually redeemed, forgiven, loved and fruitful for her husband.[385] Gomer, along with many other women

---

383   Matt. 14:8
384   Rev. 17:5
385   Hosea 3:1-3

unmentioned in this book, are clear parallels of the church.

These aspects of genuine salvation and true faith are never found in Satan's woman, as she has totally rejected God and purposefully chosen another husband. Jezebel is a good example of Satan's queen. God himself declares of her, 'I have given her time to repent of her immorality, but she is unwilling.' Just as the true Bride of Christ brings 'good, not harm all the days of her life,'[386] so Satan's bride brings the opposite: death and evil during her reign.

Jezebel

1 Kings 21:25 There was never a man like Ahab, who sold himself to do evil in the eyes of the LORD, urged on by Jezebel his wife.'

Everything about Jezebel was evil. She originated from a wicked place, she worshipped an evil god, and she killed anyone who disagreed with her. The followers of her religion were fanatics who, like her, were prepared to use violence as a means of achieving their cultic end. She seized property that was not hers, established her own false system of worship, promoted herself as a prophet and ruled by wielding ruthless political power. What is even worse than all these things is that she infiltrated God's people in such a way that the virus of her lies and deception soon became the established norm in the holy land of Israel. Through the Jezebel spirit God's people became puppets in her hand to be used and disposed of at the whim of Satan.

---

386   Prov. 31:12

Jezebel Thrives Today

Rev. 2:20 'You tolerate that woman Jezebel, who calls herself a prophetess. By her teaching she misleads my servants.'

Jesus warned his church in advance that Satan's false prophetess would attempt to infiltrate the church. She has been so successful in some denominations that many in the church don't care, or are not even aware of her presence. Her influence is obvious to see and real believers must resist it and refuse to tolerate her. The Jezebel spirit must never be allowed influence in the church, and it should be noted that this spirit can operate through both men and women.

Christ tells his Bride that through the Spirit 'his anointing teaches you about all things.'[387] One of Jezebel's primary areas of manipulation is through false teaching. Her deceitful spirit sometimes controls entire churches by teaching things contrary to the Bible or by adding things that are not contained in God's word. Jezebel's lies often give great detail about things not even mentioned in the scriptures, which mislead many.

Jezebel also claims to be a prophetess and she may appear to have access to supernatural power. This should not be surprising when considering that the works of Satan himself are 'displayed in all kinds of counterfeit miracles, signs and wonders.'[388] The scriptures continually warn the church that in the last times there will be many false prophets, and today they are popping up everywhere. Just as the daughter of Herodias was a talented dancer, Satan's lady is often exceptionally gifted, but her inner motives are unclean. Jezebel looks great on the outside and her hair and

---

387   1 John 2:27
388   2 Thess. 2:9

make-up are always immaculate.[389]

Jezebel and her offspring seek position, titles and power and are prepared to use their considerable abilities in order to obtain their selfish ambition. Despite clear warnings from Jesus, many believers are lead astray by Jezebel's talents. Such deceived people fail to heed his advice to examine the fruit of a person's life and character and not be deceived by platform showmanship. Sadly, many Christians become unhealthily obsessed with spiritual superstars who are incredibly talented and operate spectacular spiritual gifts. Jezebel relies on this naivety in order to control and influence whole groups of people.

She aims to destroy anyone who stands in her way. She killed Naboth when he would not give her his property[390] and she slaughtered the LORD's prophets when they opposed her idolatry.[391] Beware of anyone who claims that they have authority to destroy good people as part of their ministry. Paul was clear that his God given authority was for building the church up and not for tearing it down.[392] Jezebel's evil power must not be underestimated. Even Kings and prophets were afraid of Jezebel, as her spirit polluted an entire nation. Her activities can destroy an entire fellowship of believers if left unchallenged, as the church at Thyatira discovered to their cost.

A church operated by a Jezebel spirit will soon move into becoming a political system of control instead of allowing true worship amongst the believers. Instead of liberty and freedom, there will be a climate of fear.

---

389   2 Kings 9:30
390   1 Kings 21
391   1 Kings 18:13
392   2 Cor. 10:8

Through Jezebel's influence the body of Christ will be corrupted into a form of corporate organisation rather than a living organism. False methods of worship will subtly be introduced, with the end result being a form of idolatry. People's devotion will be fixed to objects and controlled by methods, instead of being submitted to the leading of the Spirit of the LORD and his word. Sadly, for many, the deception will be complete and like their counterparts in the Old Testament, they will falsely assume they are worshipping the LORD whilst actually adoring Baal's golden calf.

However, in the midst of Jezebel's wickedness, even when the mighty Elijah was afraid of her tyranny, the LORD still reserved for himself a faithful remnant of loyal subjects.[393] Likewise, the true believers at the church in Thyatira did 'not hold to her teaching and had not learned Satan's so-called deep secrets.'[394] Finally, a new King was anointed who came and threw Jezebel down from her lofty tower and the earth was rid of her.[395] The faithful believers of God will always be rescued when the true King appears. The true Bride of Christ will never follow Jezebel or bow the knee and kiss Baal; she will only worship her true Bridegroom.

Athaliah

2 Chron. 22:10 'When Athaliah...saw that her son was dead, she proceeded to destroy the whole royal family of the house of Judah.'

Athaliah may have been a queen even more wicked than Jezebel. She was the only woman to ever rule solely in her own name over the house of Judah. When her means of control came under threat through the loss of

---

393   1 Kings 19:18
394   Rev 2:24
395   2 Kings 9:32-33

her son, she ruthlessly embarked upon a genocidal campaign against the surviving children of David. The reign of terror commenced when she seized the royal throne, and it would last around seven years. Athaliah's lust for absolute power would not be satisfied until all competition to her dictatorship was exterminated. She claimed infallibility and recognised no one else's authority except her own. Despite the certainty of coming judgement she boasted, 'I sit as queen; I am not a widow and I will never mourn.'[396] With Athaliah on the throne, Satan's woman was dominating the kingdom of Judah. If she was successful in her demonic plan the seed of David, the bloodline of Messiah, could have been eliminated and the hope for the world ended. Even as her own pride led her to believe in her own success and self-importance, she had underestimated the power of God's secret weapon. The power of God's mystery is always unveiled in the time of greatest darkness. The false woman is no match for the true Bride.

2 Chron. 22:11 'Jehosheba, the daughter of King Jehoram and wife of the priest Jehoiada, was Ahaziah's sister, she hid the child from Athaliah so she could not kill him.'

Jehosheba was a royal princess, daughter of the true king, sister to the last ruler, and wife of God's high priest. She was God's woman for the hour, the bride who would save the day and continue the life of the true king on earth. She is unique in scripture being wife of God's priest, daughter to the King and sibling of the king's son. She represents the church, who is the Bride of Christ the High Priest, daughter of God the Father,

---

396   Rev. 18:7

with the DNA of God's son by the Spirit. Jehosheba would not allow the false woman to exterminate the life and testimony of the real king. She protected and hid the king, along with his nurse in the temple, so that they were kept out of the clutches of Athaliah.

Jehosheba means, 'God keeps his oath,' and even during the evil darkness of Athaliah's rule, she is proof that God always keeps his promises and keeps the real Bride alive. The Lord had promised that the eternal king would come from David's line and what God has said is always certain. She may have disappeared into hiding during this period of tribulation, but she would arise with the true king seven years later at his coronation. False religious systems around today will always try to exterminate the true life of Jesus and expression of faith in him. Many people may fall into false idol worship as they are deceived by Satan's harlot, but the true church of Jesus Christ will always keep alive the true testimony of God.

2 Chron. 23:12-13 'Athaliah heard the noise of the people running and cheering the King...She looked, and there was the King.'

There is a time coming soon on the earth when the false church may seem to gain the upper hand over the affairs of this world, just as Athaliah did. At the close of this age, in the end times, there will be seven years of tribulation, during which time Satan's false woman will seek to exterminate those who are of the bloodline of Messiah. It will be a time of trouble and tribulation, but the faithful will be preserved. The true king will return and Athaliah will be destroyed. Following the example of Athaliah, Satan's woman has only one destiny: she will be removed on the same day that the king is revealed, when he is given his throne over the house of David.

Babylon

Zech. 5:7-8 'There in the basket sat a woman! ... "This is wickedness."'
Zech. 5:10-11 'Where are they taking the basket?'...'To the country of Babylonia.'

In scripture, Jerusalem is portrayed as the Bride of Christ, and Babylon is the symbol of Satan's counterfeit woman. Mankind's evil practices can always be traced back to their origins in Babylon. False gods, Idol worship, man's system of government, evil religion, and Satan's kingdom can all be found at this city. Babylon is a fitting picture of Satan's false bride.

From Babylon's beginnings in Genesis it is always portrayed as a symbol of man's self-reliant pride and his rejection of God. Babylon continually seeks to enslave God's people and entangle them in unholy alliances and the political systems of this world. Babylon oppresses God's people and, as witnessed in the book of Daniel, it attempts to force believers to bow down to its idols and obey its corrupt system of worldly government.[397] The prophets of God all denounced Babylon and warned true believers to be separate from her. Babylon boasts that, 'I will continue forever-the eternal queen,'[398] but God says of her, 'your nakedness will be exposed and your shame uncovered.'[399]

Following her ancient and evil history of rising and falling, Babylon will

---

397   Dan.3:15
398   Isa. 47:7
399   Isa. 47:3

rise again at the end of this present age. Her final appearance on the world stage will be to enslave the earth in a marriage to her evil regime and to force everyone to submit to the devil's new world order. When Babylon appears again she is not merely described in terms of a kingdom but as a woman, she is Satan's 'Harlot.' Just as the Bride is being prepared for the coming of Christ, so Babylon is being made ready for the arrival of Antichrist.

The Woman on the Beast

Rev. 17:3 'I saw a woman sitting on a scarlet beast.'

Rev. 17:5 'This title was written on her forehead: MYSTERY, BABYLON THE GREAT, THE MOTHER OF PROSTITUTES.'

At the close of this age before the Lord Jesus returns, the world will be dominated and ruled by Satan's power. In order for Satan to set up his kingdom it is essential that he obtain a false bride in order to deceive and control people. She will have all the attributes of other evil women in scripture including Jezebel and Athaliah. This false church and evil religion will clothe itself in luxury and have great influence over the leaders of the nations. She will be responsible for persecuting and causing death to multitudes of saints and will commit blasphemy in giving herself names and titles reserved only for God. She will impose her own religious system and organisation upon everyone, which will force people to worship the devil. She will accept only her own authority and reject anyone who fails to obey and submit to her total control. Her destiny is destruction, but before her final judgement many will join in with her orgies of spiritual adultery and idolatry, and just like her will be consumed in God's wrath.

Babylon's Doom

Rev. 18:8 'She will be consumed by fire, for mighty is the Lord God who judges her.'

Babylon is doomed to destruction; Satan's kingdom and his harlot will never stand. In the providence of God, the beast and the woman who rides it have already been judged according to John's end-time vision. Whether the tower of Babel in Genesis,[400] the kingdom of Babylon in Daniel[401] or Babylon the great in Revelation, God will step in and destroy Satan's empire and the dominion of his evil bride. God declares over Babylon, 'the voice of bridegroom and bride will never be heard in you again.'[402] When God judges and destroys Satan's kingdom he also rids the earth of his false woman who has peddled his evil desires to the hearts of men. The wicked prostitute has no future and will be left ruined, naked and burned with fire.[403]

Today, God's people must recognise the full nature and reality of this false bride. There are religious organisations that are already aligning themselves to be in partnership with Satan's beast. They are totally opposed to Christ's true Bride and may attempt to destroy the concept of biblical marriage altogether These false belief systems may deceitfully claim to represent the true Bride of God, but they are the harlot of

---

400   Gen. 11:1-8
401   Dan. 5:30
402   Rev. 18:23
403   Rev. 17:16

Antichrist as Revelation 17 makes clear. This may surprise some sincere believers, as it did the apostle John, but it is true and written in God's word. True believers must have nothing to do with Satan's prostitute; they must flee Babylon and come out of her, so that they will not share in her sins.[404] When the harlot of Satan is destroyed, the true church will be protected and preserved, as it is not her destiny to suffer the wrath of God. In the new Kingdom that Christ will set up on earth, only his genuine Bride will rule alongside the True King.

---

404   Rev. 18:4

14

Incarnation Brides

'The Lord himself will give you a sign: The virgin will be with child and will give birth to a son.'

Isaiah 7:14

God prophesied in the beginning that the seed of the woman would destroy the serpent.[405] Over the ages, the prophets have confirmed that the Messiah would come at the appointed time. After the fullness of time and centuries of eager expectation, a Son was given.[406] His birth had been predicted in scripture, prophesied by the ancients and proclaimed by angels. Prestigious wise men and common shepherds came to inquire about him, but the greatest revelation of Messiah's mysterious incarnation was reserved for the women.

Jesus often gave the greatest understanding of who he was to women. He told the woman at the well that he was the Messiah, and his first appearance after the resurrection was also to a woman.[407] Unlike some

---

405   Gen. 3:15
406   Isaiah 9:6
407   John 20:14-16

of the men, the women didn't desert him at the cross.[408] Women also played an essential role at his incarnation. The presence of the woman is essential because she is a picture of his church.

At his nativity, God ensured that there were three special female witnesses who were given a unique and privileged understanding about the nature of Jesus. Each of these three brides represents an important prophetic picture to the church. Elizabeth, Mary and Anna were all brides at three different stages of marriage and each of them displayed an essential attribute of the nature of the church. When the great Bridegroom finally arrived, his Father would make sure that three brides would be present to witness and testify who he was. These women who were brides of the present, past and future would be there as representatives of all who would finally come to believe in Jesus.

Elizabeth

The Bride of the Present

Luke 1:7 'They had no children, because Elizabeth was barren; and they were both well along in years.'

When the time of God's incarnation arrived Elizabeth already had a husband, a good man named Zechariah. This woman is described as 'upright [and] blameless.'[409] Despite these positive aspects to her character, it is recorded that she had no children because she was barren. If this was not bad enough, both Elizabeth and her husband were also of an advanced age. It seemed that this bride, despite her moral and

---

408   Luke 23:49
409   Luke 1:6

righteous life, would not enjoy the pleasure of bearing children. Despite the love she received from her bridegroom, the final happiness of seeing her own children serving the Lord appeared to have been denied to her. Elizabeth stands as a representation for all God's people who have loved their bridegroom and served him faithfully, yet still feel that they have been unfruitful in some measure.

Many Churches feel this way, even in this present age; they have a wonderful bridegroom who they have served to the best of their capacity, but still have prayers unanswered. Perhaps like Elizabeth they console themselves by assuming that their prayers may be fulfilled 'in the afterlife,' but God always plans something even better for the bride who trusts in him. Despite her natural circumstances, Elizabeth's faith in God and relationship to her husband meant that she would receive her answer in the present. Unbeknown to her, God had already dispatched an angel to speak to her husband as he served his LORD in the temple. The barren bride who belongs to God can sing for joy even in the present.[410]

Luke 1:13 'Zechariah, your prayer has been heard. Your wife Elizabeth will bear you a son.'

Through God's empowering word her husband would make her fertile and Elizabeth would give birth to a son. Perhaps even greater than her own answered prayer, was that she would see, and play a part in confirming, the arrival of God's Son and Israel's saviour. She may have felt like abandoning hope during the long years of patient waiting and she may not have fully understood what her husband was trying to tell

---

410   Isaiah 54:1

her about the coming birth, but she knew Zechariah had changed and that new life was going to be birthed in her. God does not only want to create new brides, but he loves to impart fresh life to old ones as well. Too many churches think they are past it when God has planned something new for them to birth.

Elizabeth's name means 'the Oath of God.' Like Elizabeth, if churches maintain their relationship with the bridegroom, God will hear their prayer and keep his promise. If his people continue to obey his word and remain in him, then fruitfulness for the Bride is always the final outcome.

Elizabeth would receive God's promise during her lifetime and would shortly exclaim 'In these days he has shown his favour.'[411]

'Too many churches think they are past it, when God has planned something new for them to birth.'

People of God can also receive his favour today, in the present. Many years of unanswered prayer does not mean God has said no. Not only would Elizabeth bear a son, but her role would be essential in preparing the nation to receive their Messiah. Without the faithfulness of this bride birthing John the Baptist, the people would not have been ready to receive Jesus when he revealed himself. What God does today in someone's present, creates an opportunity for Jesus to come in another person's future. The church must also be faithful today in order to prepare the way for the Bridegroom to come in the future.

---

411   Luke 1:25

The Bride of the Priest

Luke 1:5 'His wife Elizabeth was also a descendent of Aaron.'

Elizabeth also represented something else of essential importance. She belonged to the tribe of the high priest and the bride of the high priest had a special dignity and purity associated with her in the Bible. The wife of the high priest could not be divorced, defiled or widowed.[412] She was highly regarded and specially consecrated. In her barrenness, Elizabeth may not have felt special but God thought otherwise. God did not just look at Elizabeth, he also saw her husband at work in the temple performing the duties ordained for him by the Lord. He always sees the man and wife together as one flesh. God would speak to this priest and answer the prayer of Zechariah in the temple.

It is the same for the Bride Christ today. The church belongs to God's high priest and has a special consecration through her covenant relationship to him. The church will never be widowed, defiled or divorced by her husband who is interceding in the heavenly temple. Jesus is the great High Priest who lives forever.[413] The fruitfulness of today's Bride is not dependent solely upon her own prayers. Her Bridegroom also intercedes for her from within the temple in heaven. His prayers from within eternity will always be heard, and his Bride will bear fruit in the present.

---

412   Lev. 21:14
413   Heb. 7:21

Anna

The Bride of the Past

Luke 2:36 'Anna…was very old; she had lived with her husband seven years after her marriage, and then as a widow until she was eighty-four.'

Anna's husband had passed away. She was not married at the incarnation and unlikely to become married in the future, she represents the bride of the past. Anna had been married for seven years but was now a widow who knew that God had done great things for her in the past. Everything concerning Anna's life is written as a prophetic picture of God's plan for his Bride. Whilst she stands as a reminder of God's historic faithfulness, she also points forward to the future of his promised provision for his Bride. She did not belong to the tribe of the king, or the tribe of the priests. She belonged to Asher, one of the least significant of the lost tribes. Nevertheless, all the hidden tribes are important to God and none of his brides, even those of the past, are forgotten by the Lord.

Luke 2:37 'She never left the temple but worshipped night and day, fasting and praying.'

Anna sums up the most commendable virtues of the brides of the past. She is a woman of God; full of faithfulness and character. Everything known about this woman is to be praised. She stands as a direct representative of all the great brides of the Old Testament who had longed to see the arrival of the perfect Bridegroom. Despite acknowledging that she was in her twilight years, Anna's zeal for the coming king was astounding. She did not wander about complaining that things were better in the old days,[414] instead she pressed on to see the glory that was yet to come. She worshipped night and day. Despite life seeming more difficult than the blessings she had enjoyed in her youth, nothing was going to prevent Anna from worshipping the lover of her soul.

There are many saints of God following her example today. Despite ageing congregations and difficulties in accepting modernity, many churches have learned the lesson of Anna. These godly saints may not have the most up to date music or modern facilities, but they know how to worship Jesus. Through their lifetime of worshipping God, many older believers have also learned how to pray despite life's difficulties. Satan fears nothing more than when a battle-hardened prayer warrior gets down on her knees. He knew that Anna was not afraid of him and he could not touch this bride who lived in the protection of God's temple. Like her namesake in the times of the Judges, Anna was going to obtain what she fasted and prayed for, and God would make sure she saw the answer with her own eyes.

The church of tomorrow needs the church of yesterday. Mary's future needed to be strengthened by the prayers and prophecy of Anna's past; without the prayer warriors of yesterday the bride of tomorrow may be overwhelmed. Anna came to encourage Mary just when she needed it; the older bride must encourage the younger church. The young believers must honour the aged saints; a time will come when they will need to rely on their inner strength. Anna 'was looking forward to the redemption of Jerusalem'[415] and she could now see it through young Mary's faith. The

---

414   Eccl. 7:10
415   Luke 2:38

baton of continuing the faith into the future had to be passed on and Anna was there to fulfil the role. 'She gave thanks to God and spoke about the child to all.'[416] She was full of positive words concerning the future and no negative comments came from her lips. Despite her age, this bride was going to serve her God and encourage the future church until her final breath.

The Bride of the Prophets

Luke 2:36 'There was also a prophetess, Anna, the daughter of Phanuel.'
Elizabeth was a bride from the priests, Mary was a bride of the kings, but Anna was from the line of the prophets. Many prophets had spoken of the Messiah's coming and there were still a few around at the time of his birth, such as Simeon. Through Anna, God would ensure that the prophetic bride was also present at the incarnation of his Son. The prophetess must be there to witness the fulfilment of the promise that was given to all the past brides in scripture. The seed of the woman had come, the promised child had arrived and all the barren women of the past would rejoice.

Everything about Anna is prophetic. Her seven years of marriage highlight the many sevens in scripture where God kept his promise to the bride. Just as Jacob had seven years before his wife was given,[417] or the Shunammite had to wait seven years before she could receive back her home,[418] so Anna's life could be measured in the seven-year cycles of the bride. She had seven years of marriage and then seventy seven being unmarried. God often speaks through his people in multiples of

---

416   Luke 2:38
417   Gen. 29:20
418   2 Kings 8:3

seven, whether it's through the seven letters in Revelation or Solomon's seven-year wait before the temple was completed. The prophetic nature of Anna is explicitly stated and the same should be observed in Christ's Bride. The Bride of Christ is a prophetic church and she should always be revealing the reality of her coming Bridegroom. The church should declare the nearness of Jesus and 'look forward to the day of God and speed its coming.'[419] The Spirit declares he is coming and so does his Bride.[420]

Anna was the daughter of Phanuel, which means 'Vision of God.' Her father appears to be named in God's word to reveal another essential aspect of Anna's nature. Anna's father declared her to be born of a Vision of God and that is what her ministry attempted to achieve. What is true of Anna should be true of the church. The Father's vision was always to obtain a prophetic Bride for his Son. The church must prophesy, and she has been empowered to do so.[421] From the birth of the church on the day of Pentecost, the Bride of Christ has had her tongue loosed and has been dreaming dreams and seeing visions. The church is never supposed to stop this, but to increase in prophetic activity as the Bridegroom gets closer. Just like Anna, the Bride of Christ should not be able to stop speaking about the redemption that is coming.

419   2 Pet. 3:12
420   Rev. 22:17
421   Acts 2:18

Mary

The Bride of the Future

Luke 1:26-27 'God sent the angel Gabriel... to a virgin pledged to be married...The virgin's name was Mary.'

Unlike Elizabeth who had already had a husband for many years, Mary was yet to be married. Although betrothed, the completion of her marriage to her bridegroom was yet to come; Mary represents the bride of the future. Mary was, no doubt, excited about her coming marriage and would have been full of hope and plans for the future. She was not of advanced age like Elizabeth, but was young and eager with anticipation for her approaching wedding day. Like all true 'women of Israel' Mary would have had strong hopes of bearing children. Being from the tribe of Judah, she may have entertained thoughts that she might have a son who would be great like one of the mighty men of her ancestor king David. It is highly unlikely that she dared to believe she would be the chosen woman highly favoured by God to birth the greatest man who ever walked the earth.

Mary is a picture of all who have a hope that God will do something great in their future. Few people may dare to think that God would choose them to carry his life in this world, but in a similar way to Mary, this is exactly what he has chosen to do. All Christians can share a similar blessing to what Mary had, because all believers are looking forward to the future hope that is coming from God. Just like Mary, true believers are eagerly awaiting their coming Bridegroom, their approaching wedding, and their future life with God. The church has the pledge of marriage, just as Mary did. God's people have the certain knowledge that God will keep his vow and that Jesus will come to claim his Bride at the appropriate time. Just as the Holy Spirit came upon Mary, God has guaranteed his oath to his Bride through bestowing the Holy Spirit upon the church, as the deposit and seal of his promise.[422]

Luke 1:29 'Mary was greatly troubled.'

Young believers in Christ often receive great promises from God. These are intrinsically connected to the divine plan that he has for their future lives. Having received promises from God many eagerly look forward to the fulfilment of the wonderful things that God has declared. Such people must, however, understand a very important aspect of the life of the Bride; she will experience trouble. Before the Bridegroom arrives, his church will go through many trials and persecutions. The severity of these difficulties will differ for each individual according to their level of faith and God's divine plan for their lives. Jesus told all believers that, 'in this world you will have trouble.'[423]

Mary understood this aspect only too well. She grasped that by allowing God's life to enter and flow through her body many people would reject her. She knew the hostility towards her may become so fierce that her life could be placed in danger. By accepting God's will for her life, her future marriage and plans could all be destroyed. Mary had a choice to make that would affect her entire future. She had to decide whether God's will for her life was more important than her own plans and whether the life of Christ within her was more essential than her own safety. Every person

---

422   2 Cor. 1:22
423   John 16:33

alive today has a similar decision to make, which will affect their entire life and future destiny. The true Bride of Christ will always yield to God before submitting to any other influence. Mary made her choice and gave her confession.

Luke 1:38 '"I am the Lord's servant," Mary answered. "May it be to me as you have said.'"

The bride, who was yet to be, chose her destiny. Mary confessed that she belonged to God before all others; she leaned on God's word more than her own understanding; and she placed her faith in his word and expected it to come to pass. Once this decision had been reached and acted upon, the Holy Spirit stepped in. God requires faith and consent from his Bride, but once this is obtained he does the rest. Unseen powers would now take control of everything in Mary's life. The Holy Spirit came upon Mary and performed the miracle in her innermost being. God would appear to Joseph and explain what was happing to the bride.[424] The Angels would talk to the shepherds and also prepare things for the future though her relatives Elizabeth and Zechariah. The Lord would change heaven and earth to ensure that his word came to pass. He would ordain cosmic events to proclaim the coming of Jesus by orchestrating the stars in the heavens to herald his coming.[425] He would alter national government affairs to ensure that the bride would be moved to the correct town at the right time for Jesus to arrive. Everything would be in accordance with God's word, for Jesus to arrive.

---

424   Matt. 1:20
425   Matt. 2:2

The Bride of the King

Matt. 2:6 'But you, Bethlehem, in the land of Judah, are by no means least among the rulers of Judah; for out of you will come a ruler who will be the shepherd of my people Israel.'[426]

Mary would have known that Messiah could not be born in Nazareth. She knew that Israel's King, just as she, was from the tribe of Judah and would be birthed in Bethlehem. God would make sure that Mary would be where she needed to be, and, despite difficulties and events beyond her control, Jesus would arrive in the right place at the right time. The king had to be born in Bethlehem and God would ensure that he would be. The ancient promise to David was fulfilled when this unknown and insignificant woman gave birth. Mary possessed a royal genetic code and, combined with the activity of the Spirit of God, the virgin was with child and birthed the son who would is God incarnate.[427] Legally and genetically, God's chosen woman was the very flesh and blood of the royal line. When Jesus was born, deity became humanity, as he was both fully God and fully man. He was the legal king and the rightful heir of the many promises of God, and Mary had birthed this unique life. The Bride of Christ also has the unique life of God within her. Through a spiritual process, rather than Mary's physical experience, the church must also give birth to God's life so that Christ's blessing can be shared with others. Many would oppose this birth and other innocent lives in Bethlehem would suffer due to the cruel and evil actions of men. Mary, like Esther, would sometimes have to hide her true identity and real nature and escape

---

426   Micah 5:2
427   Isa. 7:14

for protection amongst the gentiles. Nevertheless, the life that Mary birthed would bring salvation for mankind and Jesus would also provide redemption for the bride and mother who birthed him.

Jesus would never forget Mary, even during his essential and critical mission to save the world. He would never forsake or forget this bride who had provided for his needs. As he hung on the cross, dying for the sins of mankind, Jesus still ensured that Mary's future would be secure and that she would be taken care of. One of the last things Christ said before his death was to command that this bride was looked after.[428] He instructed his most trusted and beloved disciple to care for this woman of God. The Bride is always protected by Jesus and today he still commands his Apostles to take care of his church. From the birth in Bethlehem, through her exile in Egypt, to her pain at Calvary, the bride was never in danger of being forsaken. Despite the heart wrenching agony of the cross, Mary would soon rejoice. She would live to see Jesus resurrected and alive for evermore. The Bride's future, as always, was eternally secure.

---

428   John 19:26-27

15

The Coming Wedding

'The kingdom of heaven is like a king who prepared a wedding banquet for his son.'

Matt. 22:2

*I*n concluding the story of the Bride, it has been seen that God has done everything in preparation for the coming wedding banquet. Since her creation in Genesis, the Bride has been destined to attend the wedding described in Revelation. Even when Eve was deceived, God had already planned to rescue his Bride. It has been observed that despite her many trials, God has ensured that she has been kept safe and fruitful for him. He has found her, wherever she was, and brought her to his Son. She has been accepted into his family, obtained a royal position, and will sit at his table for all eternity. The Bride of Christ is looking forward to her coming wedding.

John 2:1 'Jesus and his disciples had also been invited to the wedding.'
Rev. 19:9 'Blessed are those who are invited to the wedding supper of the Lamb.'

Jesus often spoke about the coming wedding. All are invited to the coming wedding but, as in the parable, many who should have attended did not come.[429] Jesus never married during his thirty three years on earth and only once in the Gospels did Jesus attend a wedding. When he was asked to become involved in the wedding proceedings, he responded by saying that his 'time had not yet come.'[430] Although

'All are invited to the coming wedding.'

his wedding had not yet come, Jesus performed his first miraculous sign at a marriage celebration. By this first supernatural act he prophetically pointed toward the ultimate destination of his future ministry. He knew a time was coming when he would take his Bride and have his wedding, but before this momentous event occurred very specific details had to be worked out and certain tasks had to be completed.

When the Son of God comes to take his Bride, nothing will be left to chance; it will be the greatest and most elaborately organised wedding in history. The story of the Bible unveils the mystery of the coming wedding. What God lost in Eden will be regained at Christ's wedding in heaven. The coming ceremony will follow the marriage protocol as detailed in scripture. God's wedding will not follow one of the many different cultural expressions of marriage celebration found in the world today, but will follow the biblical pattern. Before the final consummation of a biblical marriage, specific duties of both Bride and Groom had to be fulfilled. Christ and his disciples must also ensure that they fulfil their

429   Matt. 22:14
430   John 2:4

obligations before the wedding day can be completed. If the duties are completed correctly then the wedding will be a success for all who are present. All must remember that Jesus said many are invited but few are chosen.[431]

Duties of the Bridegroom
Betrothal

Hosea 2:19 'I will betroth you to me forever; I will betroth you in righteousness and justice, in love and compassion. I will betroth you in faithfulness, and you will acknowledge the LORD.'

The bridegroom must betroth the bride to himself. No self-respecting woman would give herself to a man who was not first willing to fulfil the legal agreement of betrothal. Through this judicial process the future husband would promise his future bride what kind of bridegroom he would be. God has clearly stated what kind of husband Jesus will be to the church and he has written it down in the Bible for all to read. He will love the church forever and he will never leave her, forsake her or divorce her. His betrothal is done in complete faithfulness to every believer. He will always be truthful and righteous in the way he deals with his Bride. Christ's marriage will not be a mere legal process or relationship of convenience, but one of true love and compassion. No man has ever loved his bride with the passion that Jesus loves his church. Jesus has pledged his betrothal to his Bride in the hope that she will acknowledge it, accept it, and choose to belong to him.

---

431   Matt. 22:14

Purchase

Rev. 5:9 'You were slain and with your blood you purchased for God persons from every tribe.'

In scripture, brides were always purchased by their husbands. Hosea had to purchase his bride with silver,[432] Jacob with faithful service[433] and David with victory in battle.[434] The bridal price was dependent upon the value placed upon the woman. When it came to paying for the church, the price demanded was impossibly high. Humanity has sold itself to sin and committed unspeakable acts upon the earth. The violence and immorality of man had wreaked such havoc on God's creation that the reparation costs were too massive to contemplate. The question could be asked, 'who would want such a corrupted bride anyway, even if she cost nothing?' So much innocent blood had been shed over the centuries that the penalty for humanity's atrocities could only be atoned for by someone paying the ultimate price. The payment for the Bride's sin was death. [435]Consequently, the judicial price for the Bride was set. The cost was that a perfect life must be sacrificed to atone for her sinful life. Only supreme righteousness could pay for the Bride's total depravity. The Bridegroom must pay with his life. Every true believer knows that their saviour paid the price to save them with the last drop of his blood. As Paul declared, '[Jesus] loved me and gave himself for me.'[436] 'Christ loved the church and gave himself up for her,'[437] the price was paid, the church now belongs to Jesus and the Bride has been purchased.

---

432   Hosea 3:2
433   Gen. 29:18
434   1 Sam. 18:27
435   Rom. 6:23
436   Gal. 2:20
437   Eph. 5:25

Covenant

Matt. 26:27 'Drink from it all of you. This is my blood of the covenant which is poured out for many.'

After the betrothal and the purchase, there must still be a legal covenant agreed between the bride and groom before the wedding preparations can continue. There are several covenants in the Bible and all are important, but the marriage testament entered into by both parties is the most intimate and all encompassing. The covenant of marriage would only be binding if it was legally ratified by both parties.

In New Testament times to ensure the legal nature of the agreement, the bridegroom would take a cup of wine and drink from it. The wine would signify his promise 'in blood' to give himself to the one he loved. He would then give the cup to his future bride and ask her to drink from it. If she chose to do so she would agree, and enter into a legal marriage contract. The bride's decision and free-will agreement was essential for the covenant to be legal.

When the church partakes of Holy Communion, it likewise confirms that it belongs to Jesus as his Bride. When eating the bread and drinking the wine, the church testifies that she is bone of his bone and flesh of his flesh,[438] and chooses to ratify the solemn legal covenant of becoming his Bride. After the duties of betrothal, purchase and covenant had been fulfilled the husband would depart to build a house for the bride to live in. He would then be away for an undetermined period of time, expecting his bride to be ready when he returned, to take her to the wedding and to live with him for the rest of her life.

---

438   Gen. 2:23

As the perfect Bridegroom, Jesus fulfilled all his obligations towards his Bride. He betrothed, purchased and covenanted her to himself and he did it perfectly and completely. It has been confirmed by God the Father and by the Holy Spirit. He will return to collect his Bride at an unspecified date with an expectation that she will have fulfilled her obligations, in order for the consummation of the wedding to be completed. Although Jesus performed his duties so perfectly, there are still essential requirements for the church to complete in order for the marriage to be a success.

Duties of the Bride
She is Set Apart

1 Cor. 6:11 'You were washed, you were sanctified, you were justified in the name of our Lord Jesus Christ.'

Everything that belongs to God must be set apart from the things that are not his. Much of the Old Testament law is given over to help people understand this essential concept. The Lord taught his people to distinguish the difference between the Holy and the unclean.[439] When something was set apart it was referred to as sanctified and made holy for God's use. The priests, the temple, the equipment, and the furniture in God's house were all sanctified unto him and no one else could touch them.

Although all of these things were consecrated, nothing is more holy and sanctified to God than his Bride. She has been washed and made holy through the work of Christ and now she is to set apart to belong exclusively to him. All brides in the Bible would have known that once

---

439   Lev. 10:10

betrothed, they would live their life along this line of understanding. A bride would never allow anything to contaminate her purity, as she knew that her body was now reserved for her future husband. Anything that might risk defilement was to be avoided at all costs. Her life was not her own, she had been bought with a price; she was precious property to be given only as a gift to her beloved.

The church must understand the reality of her consecration, if she is to fulfil her duty towards the bridegroom. Christ's Bride is also part of his body and the temple of the Holy Spirit.[440] She is made holy and must not be contaminated. The things of this world seek to contaminate God's Bride and John reminded the church that she cannot love this world and also love God.[441] When speaking to the church James said, 'You adulterous people, don't you know that friendship with the world is hatred towards God?'[442] The Apostles were desperate to ensure that the Bride remained pure.

To ensure the Bride is kept pure, God tells his church what the contaminated things of the world are. They are, 'the lust of the flesh, the lust of the eyes and the pride of life.'[443] Jesus takes it for granted that his church understands that she cannot belong to two different masters[444] and expects his true Bride to be devoted solely to him. A church that pollutes herself is breaking her marriage covenant of consecration. She has no permission to become involved in the filth of this world and neither should she desire to do so. God sees through the excuses of some

---

440   1 Cor. 6:19-20
441   1 John 2:15
442   James 4:4
443   1 John 2:16
444   Matt. 6:24

churches in their attempt to be relevant to the world, as he knows they are just hiding their lust for the things of the world. The Bride is called to purity and holiness, and this is her obligation as part of the marriage agreement she made with her Bridegroom. Only the 'pure in heart'[445] will see God, and the eyes of his true Bride have no lust for this world but are longing to see Jesus.

She is Ready

Rev. 19:7-8 'The wedding of the Lamb has come and his bride has made herself ready. Fine linen, bright and clean, was given her to wear.'

It may seem patently obvious to everyone, but when her wedding day arrives, a good bride isn't taken by surprise; she is expecting it and is ready for the great day. One of the most essential aspects of the Bride being ready is that she is dressed for the wedding. The church has been clothed with 'garments of salvation and dressed in a robe of righteousness as a bride.'[446] She has ensured that her clothes are prepared and that nothing else in her life will interfere with her great day. She understands that even if her bridegroom came in the darkness of night he would recognise her because she would be wearing the clothes that he had provided for her. A faithful bride would never allow the beautiful wedding dress provided by her husband to become dirty or soiled.

The faithful church keeps itself pure and is always dressed in the wedding clothes that Jesus has given her. She dare not be found naked like the Laodicean church,[447] or the bride in the Song of Songs who did not get

---

445   Matt. 5:8
446   Isa. 61:10
447   Rev. 3:17

dressed and was left behind.[448] Just as Ruth wore her best clothes at night when waiting for her future husband,[449] and as Esther 'put on her royal robes'[450] for her king and bridegroom, the church is dressed in her best garments ready for Christ. Everyone familiar with Christ's teachings understands that anyone found not wearing the wedding garments would be considered as not belonging to the bridegroom. They would be ejected from the proceedings and thrown outside into darkness 'where there will be weeping and gnashing of teeth.'[451]

In the biblical wedding, the groom would not give the exact time of his arrival and he would often come for his bride at night. He would turn up to snatch his bride away to take her to the wedding feast and to continually live with him in his father's house. The husband fully anticipated that his bride would be ready for his arrival, as she knew he had fulfilled all of his obligations to her and made it clear that he was coming back for her. He knew that if she really loved him as she confessed, then there would be nothing more important in her life than being ready for him to arrive. Although he may have been absent much longer than anticipated preparing the banquet and the house, his bride would know that he would keep his word to return for her. She may become sleepy or impatient in the meantime, but she would still be wise in the way she prepared for his coming. She would not become like one of the foolish bridesmaids in Jesus' parable who were not prepared and had no oil when the bridegroom returned. An unprepared bride, like those in his parable, would fail to

---

448   Song of Songs 5:2-5
449   Ruth 3:3
450   Esther 5:1
451   Matt. 22:13

respond at the bridegroom's arrival, would miss the wedding day and be shut out of the proceedings.[452]

The real Bride of Christ listens to Jesus' words and knows that he said of his return, 'keep watch, because you do not know the day or the hour.'[453] She is always watching for signs of his arrival and is listening to hear the shout, 'Here's the bridegroom!'[454] She lifts up her head when she sees the prophetic signs being fulfilled because she understands that her redemption is drawing near.[455] The church has had ample time to get ready for the coming wedding. Never in its entire history has the church had more resources at her disposal to ensure that she is fully prepared for the great day. Sincere Pastors should work like John the Baptist and prepare the church for the coming of Jesus. Like the prophet, a true minister is a steward at the wedding and 'the friend who attends the bridegroom [and] waits and listens for him.'[456] Prophetic signs are everywhere in today's world, reminding believers that Jesus will shortly arrive to claim his Bride. The wedding banquet will soon be here, the house is almost finished, and the Bridegroom is preparing to return. The true Bride understands this, and will be ready to leave at a moment's notice.

She is Taken

Song of Songs 1:4 'Take me away with you – let us hurry.'

Psalm 45:13-14 'All glorious is the princess within her chamber; her gown is interwoven with gold. In embroidered garments she is led to the king.'

452	Matt. 25:1-13
453	Matt. 25:13
454	Matt. 25:6
455	Luke 21:28
456	John 3:29

The final act of the Bride of Christ on earth is that she is taken to be with her Bridegroom. In scripture, it was always prophesied that the day would arrive for the Bride to be taken into the king's chambers. Every true bride in the Bible was taken to the bridegroom, and Jesus is coming to take his church to be with him. This is one of the essential doctrines concerning the purpose and future of the church. He will take her away via the wedding banquet to the father's house for the final consummation. That has always been his intention for the Bride since she was chosen in him before the foundation of the world. The divine plan was always for the Father to provide a Bride for the Son. Everyone reading these words will choose to either be taken as the Bride, or to be left behind. The ultimate position and final condition of every living soul depends upon their response to the call of the Bridegroom.

Many people get caught up in arguments concerning the specific nature and timing of the 'rapture' and second coming of Jesus. They often view this event as a theological exercise to be debated and analysed. Some people behave more like wedding planners than the Bride. The Angels will sort out the organisational details of the wedding banquet and Jesus will arrange the seating order.[457] The church's primary role is to fulfil its obligations of being prepared and inviting other people. Those who love the Lord don't get concerned about minor technicalities, as they are too busy preparing the essentials. Having read the Bible and come to know the Lord, they understand that they are called to be his Bride and are chosen to be a part of his beloved church. They know that they are set apart unto God and must be prepared for his return; whenever that

---

457   Luke 14:8-10

event takes place. His Bride knows he is coming and nothing is going to prevent them from making sure they are ready to depart when he comes to take them. Believers who are ready and willing to go eagerly await the day when they 'will be caught up…in the clouds to meet the Lord in the air.'[458] They know that after they are taken from this realm they will be united with Jesus and live with him for all eternity.

Consummation

Rev. 21:9 '"Come, I will show you the bride, the wife of the Lamb." And he carried me away in the Spirit.'

At the end of this age in the book of Revelation, John sees a picture of the Bride living in heaven with God and reigning with him forever. Much of what he described is difficult for people to understand. Even at her final consummation, the Bride is still surrounded by an aura of mystery and it has been so from the beginning. The mystery of the woman is such a profound thought from the divine mind of God, that all eternity might not unravel its complexity. John is attempting to give an understanding about eternal things, which for people limited to earth's space and time dimensions, is hard to understand. The mystery of a man with his bride has always been too amazing to understand.[459]

What is clear is that the Bride will finally be united with Christ. What Eve lost in the garden, the church regains in heaven. God's rescue plan to regain a Bride for his beloved Son was successful. The greatest story of the ages has such a glorious ending that only God could have overseen

---

458   Thess. 4:17
459   Prov. 31:18

it. The tree of life – forbidden to be touched in Genesis after the fall into sin – is once again accessible to God's Bride. In heaven the river of life flows perpetually and God's light shines continually on his Bride.

John was so overcome with emotion at the sight he beheld that he fell down and worshipped. John saw the Bride living with the Lord and he describes the beauty of it all. Satan was finally removed from God's kingdom and a voice proclaimed that, 'There will be no more death or mourning or crying or pain.'[460] John describes the gold, jewels, glory, and honour that are all enjoyed by the Bride. His words ultimately fail to describe the joy and satisfaction that is enjoyed by the Bride when she is finally joined to her Bridegroom. She has become bone of his bone and flesh of his flesh.

John does hear the Bride speak from her royal position in heaven. She only speaks one word, 'Come!'[461] From the future of eternity the Bride beckons and invites everyone who believes to join her and belong to the great Bridegroom Jesus Christ.

---

460   Rev. 21:4
461   Rev. 22:17

Printed in the USA
CPSIA information can be obtained
at www.ICGtesting.com
LVHW010406021023
759826LV00012B/805